HOPE FOR UNITY AND DIVERSITY

How to Be a Christian, Without Being a Jerk

Derek Zahnd

Hope for Unity and Diversity:
How to be a Christian, Without being a Jerk

Library of Congress Cataloging-in-Publication Data

Zahnd, Derek.
Hope for Unity and Diversity: How to be a Christian, Without being a Jerk

ISBN: 979-8476604877
ASIN: B09GNZRNWG

Issued in print and electronic formats.

1. Christianity 2. Culture

CONTENTS

1. DIVISION

"E Pluribus Unum (Out of many, one)"

TRADITIONAL MOTTO OF THE UNITED STATES OF AMERICA, APPROVED BY AN ACT OF CONGRESS, 1782

"In God We Trust"

THE OFFICIAL MOTTO OF THE UNITED STATES OF AMERICA, ADOPTED BY AN ACT OF CONGRESS, 1956

Maybe you felt it too.

That sinking feeling in your stomach, as you watch the news. When it comes to our country, perhaps you have wondered:

- "What are we *doing*?"
- "Why are we struggling so much -- with one another?"

- "How can they *believe* that?"
- "How can they *do* that?"
- "Just where *are* we headed?"

The U.S. has seen divisiveness before.[1] In the 1850s, different responses to slavery, and a host of related issues, culminated in civil war. In 1932, we tended to divide over how to respond to the Great Depression. In 1940, we weighed different ways to respond to German aggression under Adolf Hitler. In the late 1960s, the Vietnam War divided families. In the past, we have sometimes gotten out of divisive moments through an even greater external or internal crisis. However, there is another source of hope: the citizenry. Democracies depend on the wisdom and virtue of their citizens. And that, my friend, is you and me.

And yet, you and I may not feel we are at our best. We may see ourselves on the losing side of a long string of "culture war" issues involving abortion, same-sex marriage, and the LGBTQ movement.[2] It does not help when we hear stories of Christian student groups being kicked off campus or Christians whose livelihoods were threatened for giving away a Bible, saying a prayer, or posting a Bible verse above their desk at work. We feel shocked when smeared as "bigots" or "haters" for holding the traditional Christian views that helped build our country. Even though three-quarters of Americans say they believe in God, we may sense what the Pew Research Center reports: that the percentages of Americans who say they believe in God, pray daily, and regularly go to church or religious services have all declined in recent years.[3] Meanwhile, the percentage of people who are religiously unaffiliated, the "nones", has increased.

More personally, our minds may reel from a recent series of rapid-fire, significant cultural changes. Our hearts may sting from seeing our values publicly misunderstood, maligned, and mocked. We may fear an increasingly post-Christian culture. And all this may lead us to suspect that, to a watching culture, we do look like jerks. And truth be told, in some cases - in our frustration and grief - we may have exhibited behavior that just might deserve that label. These are anxious times.

Fortunately, there is a better way.

If you have felt concerned about divisiveness in our culture, and if you identify as a follower of Jesus Christ, I invite you to think anew about how God has powerfully resourced us for just this moment. In what follows, to bring our situation into focus, we will explore examples of recent divisiveness in our country. Then we will take a fresh look at how the very nature of God speaks to what we are experiencing. That will help us remember what we are called to be and do as followers of Jesus. Finally, we will consider how all of that can shape how we engage our culture.

As we start, it is probably fair that you know a bit about me and why I wrote this book. My parents met in graduate school. My father became a professor of social work. My mother became a social worker and counselor. Growing up, our family discussed social issues. Sometimes, Christmas morning looked a little like a book exchange. In a good way.

I am a Christian. Since 1990, I have served local churches as a youth worker, cross-cultural church planter, mission pastor, and senior pastor. I am interested in the connections between theology, culture, and the mission of the church. And, I am a father. I care about the kind of culture my children and possible grandchildren will inherit. It is also important you know I have failed often - as a husband, parent, pastor, professor, and friend - at the very things I describe and recommend. I have a long way to go, and I often proceed pretty slowly. But I am convinced about the direction we need to go. As I explain in what follows, I believe this direction can help you, your church, and our culture. I am moving in this direction, and I hope you will join me.

Before discussing a solution, we will examine how the current round of divisiveness shows up in our culture. We could analyze disparate views on any number of issues including the environment, gun control, health care, criminal justice reform, human sexuality, and immigration. However, in the pages that follows we will focus on divisiveness related to the COVID-19 pandemic, racial inequality, the economy, and politics.

COVID-19

Early in the COVID-19 pandemic, national, state, and local governments began to urge citizens to adjust their lives and schedules. Initially, Americans seemed to agree on key aspects of the pandemic: at least for some, the virus was life-threatening; for the whole country, it was an economic threat; we would depend on health care and service workers to an unusual degree; the creation and distribution of vaccines would require an massive contribution from the scientific and drug manufacturing communities. However, as the pandemic unfolded, already scarce common ground eroded. According to a Pew Research Center report, "the biggest takeaway about U.S. public opinion in the first year of the coronavirus outbreak may be the extent to which the decidedly nonpartisan virus met with an increasingly partisan response."[4] In the face of a once-in-a-century challenge, Democrats and Republicans seemed to disagree about everything from where to get reliable news, to the nature and duration of shutdowns, to how to deliver education. No topic divided Democrats and Republicans more than masks[5] - except, perhaps, for whether or not to take the vaccine at all, after the effort to create, test, and distribute it.[6]

Providentially, God has seen fit to help me marry a wonderful woman who is conscientious enough for two people, although that does not let me off any hook. For this and many other good reasons, as the pandemic began, we took precautions. Yet, despite our efforts, after a few months, one of our sons and I tested positive for COVID-19. Fortunately, our symptoms were mild. Our healthcare provider directed us to quarantine at home, which we did, and eventually, we were released from their program. Curiously enough, my wife showed no symptoms. She tested negative for the virus. Living in the same home, with the virus, we had different experiences.

One year after the outbreak, the United States was divided over the handling of the coronavirus epidemic. In the summer of 2020, three-quarters of Republicans, and independents who lean Republican, felt the country had done a good job dealing with the virus. But, among those who tend to not identify with the Republican Party, less than a third felt the country had done a good job dealing with the virus.[7] Among Biden supporters, the outbreak was the central election issue: in an October 2020 poll, 82% said it was very important to their vote. Meanwhile, Trump supporters indicated the pandemic was the least significant among six issues surveyed, with just one quarter saying it was very important. More than three-quarters of American adults surveyed said that by the fall of 2020, the country was more divided than before the pandemic. Among the 14 nations surveyed, no nation was more politically divided over its government's handling of the virus than the United States.[8]

Race

I grew up and graduated from high school in a county with a very small Black population. Then I moved away to attend a large, diverse, public university. The last two years there, living with a Black roommate, were particularly enriching. Patiently and courageously, he described his experience as a Black American to me and others just beginning to come to terms with racial inequality in our country. Over the ensuing decades, relationships with people of many races continued to open my eyes to others' experiences with chronic injustice.

A series of recorded incidents of tragic police violence against Black Americans, including the killing of George Floyd, led to nationwide protests, calls for the removal of Confederate symbols, and renewed concern over racism in public life.[9] Yet Americans remain divided over the need for attention to racial inequality. From 2019 to 2020, the percentage of Black Americans who said the country has not gone far enough when it comes to Black people having equal rights with White people increased. The percentage of Hispanics saying the same also grew from 2019 to 2020, as did the percentage of Democrats and those who tend Democratic. However, in 2020, the percentage of Republicans and those who lean toward the GOP who share this opinion remained almost unchanged from the year before.

Our country is also divided on the impact we expect from attention given to race-related issues. While nearly half of American adults surveyed said the increased attention given to race and racial inequality will lead to major policy changes to address racial inequality, just over half said it will not. In the context of the coronavirus outbreak, these inequalities became matters of life and death. A Centers for Disease Control (CDC) report showed that by April 2021, more than a year into the pandemic, one of every 825 White Americans had died due to the virus, but for Black Americans, it was one of every 645 people.[10]

The Economy

When the pandemic began to make its economic impact, my attention turned to our church and our university. How would our church make it financially if our services and many of our ministries went online? How would the private Christian university where I teach and our students navigate virtual education? And then it occurred to me, what might happen to my job? What could happen to my wife's job? I am glad to say our church, university, and jobs seem to have come through all right. Nevertheless, that was not the case for everyone.

About a year after the beginning of the pandemic, there were signs of improvement in the U.S.

labor market; however, about half of non-retired adults said the outbreak will make it harder for them to achieve their economic goals.[11] The economic impact of COVID-19 hit some populations harder. Lower-income adults, adults under age 30, Hispanic Americans, and Asian Americans were among the most likely to say they, or someone in their household, had lost a job or taken a pay cut since the beginning of the pandemic. Forty-one percent of Black adults said they had taken on debt or put off bills to cover lost income.

However, higher-earning adults had a different experience.[12] Almost four in ten said their family financial situation improved in the year since the outbreak. Less than a third of upper-income adults expecting to receive government stimulus money said they planned to use it to pay bills or for something essential. Yet two-thirds of lower-income adults said they would use their stimulus funds on bills or essentials. And upper-income adults were three times as likely as lower-income adults to say they planned to save their stimulus check.

Higher earners were more likely to say that throughout the pandemic they spent less and saved more.[13] While 60% of White Americans described their financial situation as excellent or good, only 41% of Hispanic Americans and just 34% of Black Americans did so. More than three-quarters of adults with at least a bachelor's degree described their financial situation as excellent or good while only half of those with some college and just 41% of those with a high school education or less did so. While four out of five upper-income adults said they were able to continue to save during the pandemic, only half of lower-income adults said they did. Among its lasting effects, the virus revealed the depth of our economic divide.

Politics

I have family members whom I love who tend to identify with the Democratic Party. I have family members whom I love who tend to identify with the Republican Party. Presumably, in each election, some of them cancel out each other's votes.

From 1997 to 2006, I lived largely outside the U.S. Upon returning and becoming immersed again in the mainstream media, I was struck by how the knowledgeable, wealthy, and productive country I so loved could be so divided. Given all we know about the diversity of life, how could we possibly be reduced to two opposing camps? What would become of our democracy if we could not civilly discuss, debate, and ultimately decide on important issues?

Those who voted for Joe Biden and Donald Trump indicated they differed on policies, as would be expected. What may be more surprising is that a month before the 2020 election, roughly eight in ten registered voters in both groups said their differences with the other side were about core American values.[14] Roughly nine in ten – in both camps –

worried that a victory by the other would bring “lasting harm” to the United States.[15] However, large shares of Biden supporters and Trump supporters did share one sentiment: members of both groups tended to believe those who voted for the other candidate did not understand them.[16] Only 2% of Biden supporters and Trump supporters said those who voted for the opposing candidate understood them “very well”. About ten percent of each side said they felt mischaracterized by the other side, that the other side’s critique was flawed or inaccurate, and used the survey to try to tell the other side not to ascribe to them negative stereotypes.[17]

The COVID-19 pandemic, race, the economy, and politics all indicate that our culture is increasingly divided. Though ever-present, this sobering reality is a challenge to fully accept. So, for a moment, let's talk about chickens.

William Muir is a biologist at Purdue University who studies productivity in chickens. There is a sure way to measure it: you count eggs. Muir devised an experiment.[18] He selected an average flock and left it alone for six generations. Then, he created a second group of the individually most productive chickens - a super flock. Each generation, he selected only the most productive for breeding. After six generations, the average group was doing just fine. They were plump and fully feathered. Egg production had increased dramatically. However in the super flock, egg production was way down. In fact, all but three chickens were dead. They had pecked the rest to death. In the U.S., despite our economic wealth, technological advance, and political freedom, could we be pecking ourselves to death? Muir's chicken experiment may lead us to feel grateful there is one other thing on which Republican voters and Democratic voters tended to agree. Overwhelming majorities of Trump (86%) and Biden (89%) supporters surveyed in the fall of 2020 said that their preferred candidate, if elected, should focus on addressing the needs of all Americans, even if it means disappointing some of his supporters.[19]

Why Are We So Divided?

All this can leave us wondering, "How did we get *here*?" Polarizing pressures in our culture include partisan media, social media, and strain over deeply rooted cultural, historical, and regional values. We have lost a consensus on what is true. Americans divide over where we obtain information about what occurs in the world. And while Americans widely agree misinformation is a major problem, people do not see eye-to-eye about what actually constitutes misinformation. Often, one person's truth is another person's fiction.[20] Our electoral system collapses a wide range of legitimate social and political debates into a singular battle line.[21] When the margin of victory for political parties is small, as it has been in recent decades, the competition becomes cutthroat and the politics can be zero-sum. Over time, these battles result in nearly all societal tensions consolidating into two competing camps. As many have noted, divisions between the two political parties have intensified as various types of "identities" become stacked on top of political preferences. In new ways, race, religion, and ideology now align with party affiliation.

Theologian Miroslav Volf describes how we have become a culture of competing identities. He explains how the dynamics of runaway globalization produced extraordinary discrepancies of wealth and power among and within nations, including suffering and disorientation, ecological challenges, and the disruption of precious cultural, religious, and national identities.[22] In reaction, anti-globalist, nationalist, and regionalist sentiments ascended. The ensuing struggle between these forces over identity and recognition divided societies.

Volf writes, "National, ethno-cultural, religious, racial, gender, and sexual identities are major drivers of politics everywhere." Then he issues a warning:[23]

> In identity-centered struggles, religions tend to function as markers of group identities and tools in service of political forces acting as guardians of these identities. They transport the conflict [we might say divisiveness] into the realm of the sacred and heighten its stakes. That's bad for the world, above all for the people immediately affected. But that's also bad for these religions themselves ... When such religions become mark-

> ers of group identities and weapons in political struggles, they push their universal character into the background and morph into particular political religions. In monotheist versions of political religions, God becomes a servant of the group, identifying who are "us" and who are "them," whom we should befriend and whom we should colonize or destroy, whom we should exclude and whom we should embrace. This is clearly a betrayal ... a demotion of God from the Master of the Universe to a lackey of a particular group's interest.

If our country is increasingly divided, and if we run the risk of even faith-based organizations being co-opted into a polarized political struggle, how can we proceed? Where can we look for help?

2. WHAT IS GOD LIKE?

"What comes into our minds when we think about God is the most important thing about us ... Worship is pure or base as the worshiper entertains high or low thoughts of God. For this reason, the gravest question before the Church is always God Himself, and the most portentous fact about any man is not what he at a given time may say or do, but what he in his deep heart conceives God to be like."

A. W. TOZER (1897-1963)[24]

In this particularly divisive moment in the history of our democracy, any of us could feel tempted to succumb to the frightful thought that the resources available may be insufficient to sustain the social bonds that thus far have united us. Continued division and decline may be inexorable and our lot, sadly, to witness increased fragmentation, polarization, and the eventual, tragic, and painful rending of our country. This alarming possibility is worth contemplating. Nothing guarantees our democracy will continue. Even a casual familiarity with history reminds us: nations rise and fall. The further deterioration and eventual demise of our democracy is possible - and would bring unimaginable human suffering inside our country and outside it. However, there is an alternative to this gloomy scenario. You and I have been resourced to meet and surpass the challenges of our time by reflecting anew on the very nature of God revealed in the Bible. At a time when identity-oriented concerns vanquish the development of a diverse yet unified community, we can begin to transcend our dilemmas by revisiting how we think about God.

In many books, there is a core concept, a non-negotiable piece, from which the rest of the book flows. Understanding that *one* claim makes the rest of the book inevitable. This chapter focuses on that singularly important idea. We are going to explore the Trinity. Now, if up to this point you have considered the Trinity a musty, old belief that Christians accept with little understanding, get ready. I am going to ask you to consider Scriptural truth regarding what we can and should know about the Trinity. What we will look at, God *wants* us to know. These truths describe God's nature; they are revealed to us on purpose. The church has accepted these truths for centuries. So stick with me. A lot hangs on this. It will be worth it.

Most of us think of God as One, and we should. After all, Deuteronomy 6:4 declares "Hear, O Israel: The Lord our God, the Lord is one."[25] Yahweh is Israel's God. Israel was to serve and worship only Yahweh.[26] This verse is known as the *Shema*, from the Hebrew word for "hear". It presents the basic confession of faith in Judaism. And there is something agreeable to us about thinking of God as One.

However, if this is the *only* way we think about God, we can overlook the revelation in Scripture of the Triune nature of God. If Scripture describes God as One, Scripture also describes God as Three. If the Trinity demonstrates that unity and diversity are equally foundational to the very nature of God - and below I hope to show they are - and if Scripture calls us to be somewhat like God - and it does - then we have a powerful guide to shape how we think about ourselves and how we engage others. Let us begin by looking at how this unfolds in Scripture.

In The Old Testament

We see the dawn of this line of thinking in the hints of plurality in God in the Old Testament.[27] In Genesis 1:1 we read the well-known phrase "In the beginning God created." Behind God is the Hebrew term *Elohim*, a plural term for God that appears more than 2,500 times in the Old Testament and may refer to the plurality of persons in the Trinity. According to Genesis 1:26, God said, "Let us make mankind in our image, in our likeness." What meaning should we make from the plural verb, "let us", and the plural pronoun, "our"? Theologian Wayne Grudem points out some suggest they are "plurals of majesty", using a form of speech kings might employ. But there are no Old Testament Hebrew examples to support this. Others suggest God may be speaking to angels, but angels did not participate in the creation of man, nor was man created in the image and likeness of angels. According to Grudem, the best explanation may be that in the first chapter of Genesis we already have an indication of the plurality of persons in the nature of God. He writes, “We have nothing approaching a complete doctrine of the Trinity, but it is implied that more than one person is involved.”[28]

Something similar can be said of the following texts:

- Genesis 3:22 - “And the Lord God said, “The man has now become like one of us, knowing good and evil.”
- Genesis 11:7 - “Come, let us go down and confuse their language so they will not understand each other.”
- Isaiah 6:8 - “Whom shall I send? And who will go for us?”

Also, Proverbs 8 describes Wisdom as a person who does things God does.[29] More than a metaphor, here Wisdom cries aloud, hates and loves, advises and instructs. Wisdom is identified with and yet remains distinct from God.[30] In Isaiah 63:10 we read that God’s people “rebelled and grieved his Holy Spirit”, suggesting that the Holy Spirit is distinct from God himself. That it is “his Holy Spirit”, and that the Holy Spirit can be “grieved,” suggests emotional capabilities characteristic of a distinct person. In Malachi 3:1-2, the one speaking, “the Lord Almighty”, distinguishes himself from “the Lord you are seeking”, suggesting distinct persons who are both called Lord.[31]

The Old Testament points to plurality in the very nature of God. This has implications for how we understand ourselves as individuals living in community. But before we examine those implications, let's consider New Testament evidence about the nature of God.

In The New Testament

It is even easier to see evidence for the Trinity in the New Testament.[32] Because the New Testament begins with the coming of the Son of God to earth, it is not surprising that in it we see explicit teaching about the Trinitarian nature of God. As we consider New Testament texts, see if you can identify one, two, or even three members of the Trinity in these passages. Matthew 3:16-17, for example, mentions all three members of the Trinity:

> As soon as Jesus was baptized, he went up out of the water. At that moment heaven was opened, and he saw the Spirit of God descending like a dove and alighting on him. And a voice from heaven said, "This is my Son, whom I love; with him I am well pleased.

Here, three members of the Trinity perform distinct activities. God the Father speaks from heaven; God the Son is baptized and then spoken to from heaven by God the Father; and God the Spirit descends from heaven to rest upon and empower Jesus for ministry. Additionally, at the end of his earthly ministry, Jesus commanded the disciples to "go and make disciples of all nations, baptizing them in the name of the Father and of the Son and of the Holy Spirit" (Matthew 28:19). The names Father and Son and Holy Spirit indicate distinct persons. When "the Holy Spirit" is used in the same expression and on the same level as the Father and the Son, it is difficult to not conclude that the Holy Spirit is of equal standing with the Father and the Son.

Early in church history, we find evidence for the Trinity. Between 52 AD and 62 AD, Paul wrote to the believers in Philippi "Jesus Christ is Lord, to the glory of God the Father" (Philippians 2:11). And between 90 AD and 110 AD, John's gospel was written so "that you may believe that Jesus is the Christ, the Son of God, and that by believing you may have life in his name" (John 20:31). John describes Jesus as the Son of God. God is his Father. He is the Christ, the One anointed with the Spirit. Even the most basic call to believe in Jesus Christ is an invitation to a Trinitarian faith. If we start with the Jesus of the New Testament, we end up with the Triune God.

When we understand that New Testament authors generally use the name "God" (*theos*)[33] to refer to God the Father and the name "Lord" (*kurios*) to refer to God the Son, then it is clear there is a Trinitarian expression in 1 Corinthians 12:4-6:

> There are different kinds of gifts, but the same Spirit distributes them. There are different kinds of service, but the same Lord. There are different

> kinds of working, but in all of them and in everyone it is the same God at work.

Similarly, 2 Corinthians 13:14 is a Trinitarian expression, "May the grace of the Lord Jesus Christ, and the love of God, and the fellowship of the Holy Spirit be with you all." And, Ephesians 4:4-6 is as well:

> There is one body and one Spirit, just as you were called to one hope when you were called; one Lord, one faith, one baptism; one God and Father of all, who is over all and through all and in all.

All three persons of the Trinity are mentioned in 1 Peter 1:2 when describing God's elect "... who have been chosen according to the foreknowledge of God the Father, through the sanctifying work of the Spirit, to be obedient to Jesus Christ and sprinkled with his blood ..." And all three persons of the Trinity are mentioned in Jude 20-21:

> But you, dear friends, by building yourselves up in your most holy faith and praying in the Holy Spirit, keep yourselves in God's love as you wait for the mercy of our Lord Jesus Christ to bring you to eternal life.

There is plenty of biblical evidence for thinking about God as a Trinity. So it is not surprising that Christians have been thinking this way about God for a long time. It was in 325 AD, at the First Council of Nicea, and then in 381 AD, at the First Council of Constantinople, that Christians ratified their understanding of the nature of the Trinity.[34] This view of God is not important to just a few churches. Trinitarian expressions of faith, rooted in the Scriptures, continue to guide Eastern churches, Roman Catholic churches, and Protestant churches today.

This historic, orthodox view of God, and its implications for how we understand ourselves and relate to others, can help us through some of our current cultural crises. So much so, in fact, that the absence of this perspective can lead to dangerous distortions in the way we view God, others, and ourselves.

Dangerous Distortions

Based on the testimony of Scripture, if we understand God as One but not Triune, our understanding is inadequate and even dangerous. When we get things partly right in our view of God, we suffer from a distorted view and often underestimate the consequences.[35] Some distortions, called unitarianisms, develop from misunderstanding a person of the Trinity.[36]

One distortion is a unitarianism of the Creator, the first person of the Trinity.[37] God is viewed as the first principle of the universe, the origin of all - and that is correct, as far as it goes. But this distortion can also view God as the "Father Creator" of a particular ethnic or national group. Though promoting an image of Almighty God, this distortion domesticates God. Little thought is given to the work of God beyond one's own cultural, linguistic, or national boundaries.

Ethnocentricity develops unchecked. Yeah. That is not good. God is seen as the source of life, inalienable rights, and providential guidance. However, there is little awareness of sin in our relationship with God and little room for humility when we relate to people who are different from us. As a result, little thought is given to the need for repentance, forgiveness, or transformation. Historically, America's civil or implicit religion has been largely a unitarianism of the Creator.

A second distortion is the unitarianism of the Redeemer or the second person of the Trinity.[38] Jesus alone is the focus of this kind of devotion. The unitarian Jesus may be seen as a heroic personality or the central figure in worship services but has little connection to the Jesus of the Gospels and is separated from the biblical affirmation of Christ's lordship over nature and history. Salvation is defined cozily in terms of personal, present welfare while concern for justice or the environment is overlooked.

A third distortion in understanding God is the unitarianism of the Spirit, the third person of the Trinity, in which the experiences and gifts of the Spirit are primary.[39] However, insufficient effort is made to test the spirits to see if they are the Spirit of the Christ, who builds up the spiritual community commissioned to serve God and people. The impact of the Spirit of the Triune God is not merely intense religious experience, nor is it divisive or destructive to a spiritual community. The Spirit of Christ, and of the One he called Abba, works in the church, and beyond the church, empowering reconciliation, transformation, and liberation.

Each distortion reflects a current Western worship experience that falls short of the biblical description of the Trinity. Biblically informed worship is decidedly Trinitarian. John 4:23 records Jesus saying, "A time is coming and has now come when the true worshipers will worship the Father in the Spirit and in truth, for they are the kind of worshipers the Father seeks." In Ephesians 2:18 Paul wrote, "For through him [Christ] we both have access to the Father by one Spirit." In recent years, a growing number of scholars have reflected on the impact of the Trinity. For example, theologian Robert Letham reminds us, "general theistic [non-Trinitarian] worship is defective."[40] And late theologian Stanley Grenz agreed, claiming the traditional discussion of God "as a being is no longer helpful. There is no God but the Father, Son and Spirit."[41]

If failing to think about the Trinity can lead us to dangerous distortions in the way we think of God, and if true worship requires us to contemplate the Triune nature of God, let us explore the significance of what it means to think of God as a Trinity.

Thinking of God As A Trinity

Almost immediately, we are struck by the idea that thinking about the Trinity is hard. It does not come as naturally as thinking of God as merely One.

For example, we are happy to think "God is love". After all, 1 John 4:8 tells us so, and it is comforting to remember God loves us. However, as we will explore, before Scriptures like 1 John 4:8 were inspired, and before humans were created and could be loved, God was love as divine persons in other-preferring relationships within the Trinity. While it is easier for us to think, "God is love" than "God is a Trinity", God is love precisely *because* God is a Trinity, a community of divine persons in perfect, loving relationships.[42]

We may struggle to think about the Trinity because the word never appears in the Bible. For Christians who take the Scriptures seriously, this does not sound good. It has even given rise to a suspicion that the concept of a Divine Trinity is the invention of ancient theologians with too little to do. That suspicion withers, however, in light of the passages described in the New Testament section, above. The idea that God is a Trinity is derived from the descriptions of God by the people of God recorded in Scripture.

Another reason we struggle to think of God as a Trinity is failed illustrations.[43] Someone will say, "The Trinity is something like an egg: a shell, a yolk, and the white. And yet it is all one egg." Another will say, "No, the Trinity is more like clover: three bits stick out, like the Father, Son, and Spirit, but it is still one leaf." Yet another will say, "No, the Trinity is like the three states of water: solid, liquid, and gas. It takes on different forms, but it's all water." Comparing the Trinity to eggs or leaves or water or even rehearsing what the Trinity is not - it is not three Gods - may help us feel we are taking a stab at orthodoxy, but it does not make much practical difference to our lives or our world.

So, if we are going to give this a whirl, how should we even *try* to think of the Trinity? Wayne Grudem writes, "God eternally exists as three persons, Father, Son, and Holy Spirit, and each person is fully God, and there is one God."[44]

God is three persons:

- The Father is not the Son; they are distinct (John 1:1-2, John 17:24, 1 John 2:1, Hebrews 7:25).
- The Father is not the Spirit; they are distinct (John 14:26, Romans 8:27).
- The Son is not the Spirit; they also are distinct (Matthew 28:19, John 16:7).[45]

Each person in the Trinity is fully God:

- God the Father is fully God (Genesis 1:1, verses throughout the Old Testament and New Testament, Jesus' many prayers to his Father in heaven including Mark 15:34 and Luke 23:24).
- The Son is fully God (John 1:1-4, John 20:27-31, Hebrews 1, Titus 2:13, Romans 9:15, Colossians 2:9, Isaiah 9:6).
- The Spirit is fully God (Matthew 28:19, Acts 5:3-4, 1 Corinthians 3:16, Psalm 139:7-8).

Many of us are familiar with God's attributes: God is eternal, omnipresent, omnipotent, omniscient, utterly wise, entirely holy, infinitely loving. However, we may tend to associate these attributes with God the Father, more than with God the Son or with God the Spirit. The biblical teaching on the Trinity is that God's attributes are true of each Triune person, Father, Son, and Spirit because each person is fully God.[46] Starting from another place, another way to say this is there is one God. The three persons of the Trinity do not just think alike or share the same purpose, they have one essential nature (Deuteronomy 6:4-5, Isaiah 45:5-6, Isaiah 45:21-22, Romans 3:30, James 2:19).

Theologian Daniel Migliore reflects on the Trinity: [47]

> The distinctively Christian understanding of God as ineffable mystery of love who is one in essence but distinct in three eternal "persons", Father, Son, and Holy Spirit. The three are differentiated only by their relations to each other as Begetter, Begotten, and Breathed Forth ... The three equal persons are united in an eternal movement of utterly singular mutual self-giving love so intimate as to be an in "indwelling' or "in-existing" of each other.

Now at first, all of that may seem biblically true, but a bit abstract. However, given our cultural challenges, bringing the doctrine of the Trinity to the front of our minds is actually surprisingly helpful. We are not far removed from universalizing traditions that exalt the one over the many, view multiplicity unfavorably, and tend towards totalization and globalization.[48] Just reflect on historically recent experiences with runaway fascism and socialism. From a Trinitarian perspective, tyranny, in which one person or small group dominates and exploits others, suppressing human dignity and liberty, is heresy.[49] Unity triumphs, but at the expense of diversity. While cultural winners may be celebrated, elements of the culture are weakened or killed. On the other hand, pluralizing perspectives prefer the many to the one, discount unity, and prescribe de-totalization, decentralization, differentiation, and individualization. From a Trinitarian perspective, in the extreme, this reflects the heresy of Tritheism. Factions break away, form their own power bases, and pursue their own ends. This multiplies rival power centers and furthers the breakdown of social cohesion. Diversity rules, but unity is destroyed. People may be free to do their own thing, but have so few things in common that freedom is curtailed. In both cases, the losses exceed expectations. Thinking in Trinitarian terms, however, offers an escape from the one-many dichotomy because, if unity and diversity are both inherent in the nature of the Triune God, then God is the ground for both. The one does not dominate and neither do the many. When it comes to cultural categories, only unity in diversity can correspond to the Triune God.

If a Trinitarian understanding of God is so promising for us, it certainly deserves a closer look.

Let's examine what just one aspect of the Trinity could mean for you and me and our relationships with others.

Mutual Indwelling

John 14:10 records Jesus saying something that stretches our minds in a Trinitarian direction:

> Don't you believe that I am in the Father, and that the Father is in me? The words I say to you I do not speak on my own authority. Rather, it is the Father, living in me, who is doing his work. Believe me when I say that I am in the Father and the Father is in me.[50]

To capture what we are seeing in Scripture I want to introduce you to a new word. Descriptions of personal interiority within the Trinity – "I am in the Father and the Father is in me" - have given rise to the idea of *perichoresis*. Perichoresis is a Greek word that can be translated "mutual indwelling". Originally, it was used to describe the way the divine nature and human nature indwell Jesus Christ. In the eighth century, Eastern theologian John of Damascus used the term to describe the unique communion of the Trinitarian persons. Perichoresis advances the idea that "the three persons of the Trinity live in, with and through one another."[51]

It may be helpful here to also note the theological term "appropriation".[52] Following biblical passages, theological appropriation ascribes a particular attribute or act to one of the Triune persons, even though the attributes and acts of the Trinity are indivisible and cannot be assigned solely to one person. For example, creation is often appropriated to the Father, redemption is often appropriated to the Son, and sanctification is often appropriated to the Spirit. Strictly speaking, however, all three are acts of the one Triune God. While the idea of perichoresis guards the idea of the unity of the Trinity, the concept of appropriation helps retain the distinctions within the Trinity.

Now, let's get back to mutual indwelling. Miroslav Volf describes it this way:

> The one divine person is not that person only, but includes the other divine persons in itself; it is what it is only through the indwelling of the others. The Son is the Son because the Father and the Spirit indwell him; without this interiority of the Father and the Spirit, there would be no Son. Every divine person is the other persons, but he is the other persons in his own particular way.[53]

I know this is not the way we are accustomed to thinking, and it can seem fuzzy. But consider this example. Using the idea of perichoresis, some conceive of the Trinitarian persons as united in an exquisite dance. And today, we hear an echo of the Greek word perichoresis in our English term choreography.[54] Thoughtful Christians have expressed the persons of the Trinity as making room for one another, being unimaginably hospitable to one another, being in one another, encircling one another, and pervading one another.[55] This perfect, mutual indwelling demonstrates peaceful mutuality, reciprocity, cooperation, and unity in genuine diversity.[56]

Because the Triune God is characterized by both unity and diversity, it is not surprising that unity and diversity are showcased in the beauty of creation. Think about it. We see unity in diversity in the harmonious working of diverse systems in the human body: our respiratory, circulatory, nervous, and digestive systems, among others. We see unity and diversity in the interconnectedness of the earth's environmental systems: geosphere, biosphere, cryosphere, hydrosphere, and atmosphere. We see unity and diversity in biblical marriage (Genesis 2:24). God created people, male and female, with differences that can be united in mind, body, and spirit. We see unity and diversity in complex musical compositions, bird migration practices, work teams, and athletic teams. As I wrote this, the New York Yankees pulled off a major league baseball record-tying third triple play of the season.[57] At this example of unity in diversity, Yankee players and fans reacted in spontaneous joy. Throughout creation, God uses unity in diversity to display his glory. And, as we will see below, in the complex composition and manifold ministries of the local church, he still does.

Given the extremes we have seen in recent years, with unfettered globalization, on the one hand, and then ascendant nationalism, regionalism, and identitarianism, on the other, understanding God as the foundation of unity and diversity can give us a stable place to stand as we consider who we are and how to engage one another.

Now it also makes sense that we consider how power affects relationships among Trinitarian persons. During most of the history of the doctrine of the Trinity, hierarchy in the Trinity was the uncontested view. Hierarchy was also largely uncontested in human communities. Within the Trinity, it was thought that the Son was subordinate to the Father. The primacy of one person seemed necessary for the unity of the three persons in the Trinity and for their distinctions. From this perspective, egalitarian or social understandings of the Trinity appear as a projection onto God of modern, democratic sentiments. However, it is not clear that hierarchy would be necessary to guard either divine unity or the distinctions among divine persons. Volf writes, "in a community of perfect love among persons who share all divine attributes a notion of hierarchy is unintelligible." In fact, from this perspective, hierarchical constructions of Trinitarian relations appear as projections of earthly hierarchies onto divine persons, possibly driven by nostalgia or fear.[58] In any case, this presentation adopts an egalitarian or social Trinitarian perspective.[59] In this view, the mutuality and relationality of the Trinity suggest radical human equality. The Trinity provides cultural critique resisting structured inequality in all spheres of life, whether between the two sexes, in politics, or in the church.[60]

As you can see, how we think about the Trinity can have significant implications for how we think about many other things. But before exploring that, it is important to examine the correspondence between the divine persons of the Trinity and human persons like you and me.

Trinity-Human Correspondence

Genesis 1:26-27 teaches us that human beings are made in the image of God.[61] Volf suggests that an image (in this case us), which is not supposed to reflect the reality of which it is an image, would be strange.[62] It is hard to conceive of a mirror that does not reflect what it faces. He also suggests it would seem odd to claim that human beings, who are created for communion with the persons of the Trinity and who are "created to be like God" (Ephesians 4:24), should not seek to be like God in their mutual earthly relationships. Scripture reminds us: God's earthly children should be like their heavenly Father (Matthew 5:45). Jesus commanded his disciples, "Be perfect [*teleios*; complete, not lacking], therefore, as your heavenly Father is perfect [*teleios*; complete, not lacking]" (Matthew 5:48). The nature of God, then, should shape the character and the behavior of people who worship God.[63]

In the life of the church, the Trinity-human correspondence proceeds from conversion, when the

Spirit regenerates and indwells a person (Titus 3:5, 1 John 4:15), to baptism in which people identify with the "name of the Father and of the Son and of the Holy Spirit" (Matthew 28:19) to the after-life where communion with the Triune God is consummated.[64] Throughout church life, the relations within the Trinity correspond to the church because the Triune God is present in each person who makes up the church through the indwelling Spirit, shaping the church in the image of the Trinity.[65] Within the church, just like within the Trinity, people cannot live in isolation.[66] The symmetry and reciprocity of the relationships among the Trinitarian persons correspond to the church in which all members, not just officeholders, serve one another with Spirit-given gifts, imitating the Lord Jesus Christ, to the glory of God the Father. Volf reminds that, "like the divine persons, [Christians] all stand in a relation of mutual giving and receiving."[67] The Trinitarian persons are a community of perfect, self-donating lovers, in which:

> the self gives something of itself, of its own space, so to speak, in a movement in which it contracts itself in order to be expanded by the other and in which it at the same time enters the contracted other in order to increase the other's plenitude.[68]

On the cross, Jesus Christ supremely translated Trinitarian self-donation into our world in the power of the Spirit to the glory of the Father. Therefore, relationships among human beings indwelt by the Spirit of God will be characterized by voluntary self-contraction and other-related self-fulfillment.

Limits To Trinity-Human Correspondence

Now I know what you may be thinking. Any of us could be quick to point out - after driving our highways, watching the news, or parenting - there are limits to the Trinitarian-human correspondence. Humans are not divine. Not by a long shot. First, human perception is limited. So is language. Human notions of the nature of the Triune God cannot express precisely who the Triune God is.[69] Humans are created. We can only correspond to, or be like, God in creaturely ways. Trinitarian persons mutually indwell one another in ways that human persons do not. Trinitarian relationality is perpetual, yet human relationality must be nurtured voluntarily. And Trinitarian concepts such as "persons" and "relations" are analogies themselves and can only be applied to humans in analogous ways.[70]

But also, humans are sinners (Romans 3:23). In our earthly lifetimes, humans will not be made into the perfect creaturely images of the Triune God we are destined to become. And humans live in the created world. We are deeply affected by the beautiful, complex, and yet oh-so-fallen cultures in which we live. While there are analogies between the Trinitarian persons and human persons, we must always remember: they are weak analogies. The Trinitarian cycle of perfect, reciprocal, self-donating love simply will not be repeated by human relationships in our broken world. The mutually-indwelling unity and perfect love experienced in the Trinity are unique. The reflections of it we can hope for in the church will be broken and faint at best.[71] Such is the extent of human fallenness, that when the Word entered our world, in the power of the Spirit, sent by God the Father, to translate the delight of eternal, mutual, self-giving, divine love into a human life, that life was killed in an agony of love on the cross.[72]

So we proceed soberly and cautiously, knowing any divine-human correspondence is partial. But at the same time, we do not forget that there is a divine-human correspondence and that it is described in Scripture for our benefit. With such limits in mind, let's look at the significance of Trinitarian-human correspondence for understanding ourselves as persons in relationships.

Personhood

At this point, we have discussed that the New Testament takes for granted that there are three divine persons when it speaks of the coming of the Son to inaugurate the kingdom of the Father, in the power of the Spirit. One in essence, the Father, Son, and Spirit are different persons because of their distinct relationships to each other. We can think of them as the One who Begets, the One who is Begotten, and the

One who Proceeds. Or, we could say, following Augustine, they are the Lover, the Beloved, and the Love that issues from them and binds them together.[73] All of this means the communal relationality among the Father, Son and Spirit is the archetype of true human personhood. The idea of human personhood is grounded in the reality of divine, relational persons. Implications of this divine communal relationality are felt in all human communities, including in the church.[74] Because believing humans are indwelt by the same Spirit that also indwells the Father and Son, within the church, our identities can be stable yet porous, bounded yet permeable. Like a velvet-covered brick, we can be solid on the inside, but soft to the touch. Such porosity does not compromise our individuality but expands and enriches it.[75] We are enhanced precisely by allowing others into our lives.

Relationships

Jesus' statements like "the Father is in me, and I in the Father" (John 10:38) reveal that the Trinitarian persons are mutually internal. Because of this, the persons of the Trinity do not enter into relations with one another, so much as they are constituted by one another in their relationships.[76] Each Trinitarian person "depends" on the other Trinitarian persons for his deity. The Trinitarian persons prefer one another. For example, after the Father hands over the kingdom to the Son at the end of time, the Son hands it back to the Father (1 Corinthians 15:24) glorifying the

Father (Philippians 2:11). On the one hand, the divine community is not a collection of independent and self-standing divine persons. And on the other hand, the divine persons are not merely individual parts or functions of a community. Within the Trinity, personhood and relationship are equally foundational.[77] The Triune persons live in a beautiful community of simple love expressed in perfect agreement among Father, Son, and Spirit. We find this in the Son's deference to the Father (John 4:34; 5:30; 6:38-39). We see it in the Father's support of the Son (Matthew 3:17; 17:5). And we note it in the way the Spirit proceeds from the Father and is sent by the Son (John 15:26; 16:7).[78]

Now, this may seem inspiring but remote until we remember there is correspondence between the relations among Trinitarian persons and the relations among people in the church. The indwelling Spirit brings the fruit of God's Spirit into human lives: love, joy, peace, forbearance, kindness, goodness, faithfulness, gentleness, and self-control (Galatians 5:22-23). This same Spirit endows the people of God with spiritual gifts. The Spirit distributes these gifts universally, unconditionally, and generously throughout the church. These spiritual gifts function interdependently. This implies shared, human responsibility for the operation of the church. Full expression of the fruit of the Spirit and the gifts of the Spirit is found only in the entire, local, relational church.[79]

We have seen that people are created in the

image of God (Genesis 1:26). And we have seen that throughout eternity God has been and remains a community: the fellowship of Father, Son, and Spirit. The creation of humans in the divine image, therefore, cannot mean less than that humans express some degree of the relational dynamic of the Trinitarian persons whose representation we are called to be.[80] Sin is, among many other things then, the unfortunate destruction of human community meant to represent the image of the Triune God.[81] Community-destroying sins the Bible warns against include, but are not limited to, discord, jealousy, rage, selfishness, slander, gossip, arrogance, disorder (2 Corinthians 12:20), lying (Proverbs 12:22), adultery (Hebrews 13:4), and divorce (Matthew 5:31-32). The Triune God calls the church, even amid brokenness and divisiveness, to exemplify the ideal community of love, which is the divine essence.[82] The church begins to fulfill God's purpose when it at least partially reflects God's image.

All this has implications for what it means to be a human person. Without denying the radical differences between divine and human persons, or that the mutual indwelling of the Triune persons is an intimacy far beyond any creaturely relationship, a Trinitarian understanding of personhood and relationships questions the adequacy of individualistic views of human persons. Perspectives that equate personal life with complete autonomy and lack reference to relationships with others as constitutive of personhood are inadequate.[83] Even if God's Trinitarian nature exceeds our comprehension, it is in line with Scriptural teaching that human life created in the image of God finds its fulfillment only in loving relationships with God and with our neighbors. Migliore writes, “The Christian hope for peace with justice and freedom in community among peoples of diverse cultures, races, and gender corresponds to the Trinitarian logic of God.” Reflection on the Triune God radically questions all totalitarianisms that deny people freedom and dignity. And Trinitarian reflection resists as idolatrous individualisms that undermine common welfare. The doctrine of the Trinity describes God - a divine, loving community reaching out through inclusive love - as the source of all genuine human community, superseding claims based on race, sex, or class.[84] The life of God can be understood as the perfect, endless communion of Father, Son, and Spirit, uniquely giving and receiving love as they mutually indwell. If we, by the Spirit, with all our creaturely limitations and sinfulness, are incorporated into Christ, then it is entirely reasonable to describe the essence of the church as communion with God and communion with one another.[85]

Herman Melville, the author of *Moby Dick,* wrote, “The reason the mass of men fear God, and at bottom dislike him, is because they rather distrust his heart, and fancy him all brain like a watch.”[86] At this point, I hope you can see that the nature of the relational Triune God, as revealed in the Bible, could not be more different. What if, in deep irony, an idea we may have thought irrelevant, is after all, a vital and urgently needed source of life for God's people? A Trinitarian perspective offers a profoundly personal and relational view of God - and of the life God created and redeemed for God's people.[87]

Well, that is a lot of abstract thinking to work through. Congratulations! Now, let's switch gears and think practically about what this means for our lives. In conversation with a loved one or by writing in your journal, take some time to respond to the following questions.

Reflection Questions And Next Steps:[88]

1. Read Matthew 3:16-17. Can you identify each person of the Trinity in this passage?
2. Are there any hindrances you may need to resolve to move forward thinking about the Trinity?
3. If the Trinity is the fundamental expression of unity and diversity, what aspects of creation also show unity and diversity? Do you find people take delight in spontaneous expressions of unity and diversity? If so, why is that?
4. What emotions do you experience when you reflect on the nature of the Trinity?
5. What kind of spiritual practices could help

you develop a deep and transforming relationship with the Trinity?

6. What are some ways your family or workplace demonstrates the diversity of the Trinity?
7. In what ways does your family or workplace manifest the unity found among the members of the Trinity?
8. How might the diversity among the members of the Trinity encourage your family or workplace to allow the development of distinct interests, without threatening its unity?
9. How might the unity of the members of the Trinity challenge your family or workplace to develop unity, without hindering its members' individuality?
10. How might the unity and the diversity of the Trinity challenge your local church to express diversity in unity?
11. Is the Trinitarian nature of God more fully expressed in a church made up of people of one race or in a church composed of people of many different races (See Acts 15:1-29, Ephesians 3:1-10 and Revelation 7:9-10)?
12. How do the relationships among the persons in the Trinity inform the way you exercise authority and follow authority? How does this play out in your life at school and work, in your community, and as you relate to your government?

13. In heaven, do you think you will be just like everyone else, or will you continue to have a personality that is distinct and your own (Matthew 8:11)? In the Triune God, we have distinct personalities combined with complete unity. How can this reassure someone who might fear losing who they are as they get closer to God or closer to other people in a local church?

3. WHAT CAN THE CHURCH BE LIKE?

"My prayer is not for them alone. I pray also for those who will believe in me through their message, that all of them may be one, Father, just as you are in me and I am in you. May they also be in us so that the world may believe that you have sent me. I have given them the glory that you gave me, that they may be one as we are one — I in them and you in me — so that they may be brought to complete unity. Then the world will know that you sent me and have loved them even as you have loved me."

- JESUS, JOHN 17:20-23

Alright. We have looked at indicators of the divisiveness happening around us in our culture. And we have seen how the Trinity is the basis for personhood and relationships, a perfect community of diversity in unity. But what does this mean for you and me as we live out our lives here and now as the church?

Well, one place to start is with the member of the Trinity described as the head of the church.[89]

Jesus prayed that his followers would be one, as he and the Father are one (John 17:20-23). Let's look at part of Jesus' farewell prayer, uttered among friends at the close of a meal, anticipating his death for the salvation of all who would believe.

Jesus says, "My prayer is not for them alone. I pray also for those who will believe in me through their message" (John 17:20). Behind "prayer" is a Greek verb meaning "to ask". In Greek, the verbs *aiteo* and *erotao* can both be translated as "to ask". Aiteo more frequently suggests the attitude of a suppliant, the request of one who is lesser in position to one who is greater in position. Aiteo is used, for example, when a child makes a request of a parent (Matthew 7:9-10), when a subject makes a request of a king (Acts 12:20), and when people ask something of God (Matthew 7:7). Erotao, however, is different. Its usage suggests the petitioner is on equal footing or familiar with the person of whom he makes a request. It is a term a king would use to make a request of another king (Luke 14:32). Significantly, when making a request of the Father, Jesus Christ never used aiteo. As often as he asks, or declares that he will ask something of the Father, it is always erotao that is in use, depicting an asking upon equal terms (see, for example, John 14:16; 16:26; 17:9, 15, 20).[90] When Jesus asks something of the Father, he does so as a peer.

Jesus prays, "That all of them may be one, Father, just as you are in me and I am in you" (John 17:21). Knowing the many creaturely limitations we have, and the perfect, loving communion he experiences with the Father and with the Spirit, he still prays to the Father that the oneness of his followers will be "just as you are in me and I am in you." At one level, the Spirit has accomplished this. We are reminded in 1 Corinthians 12:13, "For we were all baptized by one Spirit so as to form one body—whether Jews or Gentiles, slave or free—and we were all given the one Spirit to drink." At another level, it falls to each generation of Christians to express this reality in our relationships.

Jesus prays, "may they also be in us so that the world may believe that you have sent me" (John 17:21). Behind "world" is a figurative use of the Greek word *kosmos* referring to people associated with a world system estranged from God.

Jesus continues, praying with emphasis, "I have given them the glory that you gave me, that they may be one as we are one" (John 17:22). Theologian George Beasley-Murray indicates that just what "glory" here refers to has led to much discussion.[91] To my mind, the indication is that glory here refers to the gift the Son of God gave through his incarnation, death, and resurrection to all who believe: a saving relationship with God.

"I in them and you in me—so that they may be brought to complete unity," Jesus prays (John 17:23). That future followers of Christ would be perfectly one is a consequence of God the Son and God the Father mutually indwelling one another.

"Then the world will know that you sent me and have loved them even as you have loved me" (John 17:23). "Them" here refers to the disciples. The absolute (*teleioo*) unity of Jesus' disciples is meant to challenge the world to acknowledge that the Father sent the Son and that the Father loves Jesus' disciples in the same way he loves the Son.[92] This is how created, sinful men and women may attain a unity with one another something like that which exists within the Triune God; or, more precisely, how we may together participate in the very unity within the Trinity.[93]

We have already pointed out it is the way God the Father and God the Son mutually indwell as persons in a relationship that determines the unity of redeemed humanity: "I in the Father and the Father in me" (John 14:10–11, 20; see also John 10:38). While this kind of unity is possible only through the accomplished redemptive action of the Son of God, it calls for an appropriate response from the people drawn into it. The people of God are to embody the revelation and the redemption of the Son of God before the world. We do this so that the world may hear that Jesus is the Christ, but also so they may see that the Son of God has the power to transform fallen men and women into the likeness of God and to bring about the kind of community for which the world longs.[94]

The basis of the unity of the church, then, is the relations within the Triune God and the reality of the ongoing, redeeming work of the Son of God on earth through the Spirit of God.[95] That unity *was realized* when the Son gave those who believed in him the glory the Father had given to him (John 17:22). In Christ, the deepest divisions of humanity have been bridged. No longer are Jews and Gentiles divided from one another by competing hopes; no longer are slaves and free separated by social status; no longer are male and female viewed as living on different levels, for all have become one in Christ (Galatians 3:28). There is no earthly chasm created by culture, tradition, or political order that cannot be bridged through Christ.

However, as we know, the fall (Genesis 3) affects even this new spiritual community.[96] Not long after Pentecost, the harmony of the early church in Jerusalem was upset through dissension between Aramaic-speaking Jewish Christians and Greek-speaking Jewish Christians (Acts 6:1). If this could happen so early in the history of the church between Christian Jews, albeit from different cultural starting points, it was bound to happen on a larger scale when the church grew to comprise people from many cultures and nations. In fact, much of the New Testament bears witness to first-century efforts to maintain the church unity won by Christ. Over fifty times New Testament authors call believers to treat one another in specific unity-building ways. (See Appendix: Select "One Another" Passages from the New Testament.) Reflecting on a sub-set of the New Testament's "one another" commands - to love one another, remain members of one another, demonstrate kindness to one another, encourage one another, serve one another, and honor one another – provides us specific, earthly ways Jesus' prayer can begin to find its answer in us. As we follow these commands in our local churches, our personhood and relationships can reflect, in weak and faint ways, the very personhood and relationships of the Triune God - that the world may perceive the reconciling power of God in Christ.

Loving One Another

"A new command I give you: Love one another. As I have loved you, so you must love one another. By this everyone will know that you are my disciples, if you love one another."

JESUS, JOHN 13:34-35

"The only thing that counts is faith expressing itself through love."

PAUL, GALATIANS 5:6B

In 1943, 230 women were arrested as members of the French Resistance and sent to Birkenau.[97] Tragically, only 49 survived, but this in itself is remarkable. These women were as diverse as could be imagined—Jews and Christians, aristocrats and working-class, young and old. Yet their commitment to the French Resistance and one another united them. Using the journals and memoirs of survivors, Caroline Moorhead reconstructs how the solidarity of these women sustained them through unspeakable horror and torture in her book *A Train in Winter*.

Many Holocaust survivors hoarded whatever scarce resources they could save for themselves. Who would blame them? Survival became the only goal—no matter the cost, even to others. Yet, in most cases with these French women in Birkenau, they demonstrated solidarity toward each other rather than the selfishness that engulfed many others. Moorhead writes, "Knowing that the fate of each depended on the others ... egotism seemed to vanish ... stripped back to the bare edge of survival, each rose to behavior few would have believed themselves capable of." When unrelieved thirst threatened to push one woman over the brink, for example, the others pooled their meager rations to provide her a full bucket of water.

Such love is rare. Human selfishness is as natural as breathing, and just as unconscious. Yet the women of the French Resistance underscore the extraordinary nature of what Christ has done. The women - having bonded through a crisis - demonstrated solidarity with one another in the face of their enemies. Yet Jesus stood in solidarity with us in human suffering and death, when we were still his enemies (Romans 5:6-11).

The beginning of John 13 describes Jesus in the context of Triune God: "Jesus knew that the Father had put all things under his power, and that he had come from God and was returning to God" (John 13:3). So Jesus

got up from the meal, took off his outer clothing,

> and wrapped a towel around his waist. After that, he poured water into a basin and began to wash his disciples' feet, drying them with the towel that was wrapped around him. (John 13:4-5)

After completing this remarkable act of service, Jesus returned to the meal to interpret the act to his followers, saying, "Now the Son of Man is glorified and God is glorified in him. If God is glorified in him, God will glorify the Son in himself, and will glorify him at once" (John 13:31-32).

Jesus' self-giving love, stemming from the inexhaustible love experienced within the Trinity, became the example and means by which the new Christian community would survive in a first-century environment that met them with apathy and hostility.[98] His command is rooted in the Old Testament (Leviticus 19:18) and is one of the two most important commands (Mark 12:28-31). In it, behind "one another" is a reciprocal pronoun *allelon*. Outside the Gospels, the word appears 58 times in the New Testament. Paul uses it 40 times.[99]

Of course, Jesus is not the only person to teach on love in the Bible. 1 Peter 1:22 reminds us, "Now that you have purified yourselves by obeying the truth so that you have sincere love for each other, love one another deeply, from the heart." And later in 1 Peter 4:8 we read, "Above all, love each other deeply, because love covers over a multitude of sins." The term behind "deeply" was used to describe the taut muscles of an athlete who strains to win a race. It describes intense and constant activity.[100] Christians are called to love eagerly, to love earnestly, and to love strenuously.[101] Peter assumes his readers' love is being tested by current trials, and that it will be tested by future trials, so he emphasizes the constant imperative that Christians love one another.[102] Peter says, in effect, if you love one another, you will always be ready to forgive other people's sins and the unfortunate things they may do to you.[103]

In Crisis

Christians are called to love one another, especially in times of crisis. The coronavirus epidemic is the most significant public health crisis of our lives, but it is not the first time Christians have faced such a challenge. Lyman Stone reviews Christian responses to past epidemics.

In the second century, the Antonine Plague may have killed off 25% of the Roman Empire.[104] Christians cared for victims out of a spiritual perspective in which plagues were not the work of angry and reckless deities but the product of a broken creation in revolt against a loving God. In the fourth century, during another plague, Roman Emperor Julian complained that "the Galileans" were taking care of people who did not agree with their beliefs. Christian historian Pontianus wrote that Christians ensured that good was done to all, not merely to the household of faith. Europe's first hospitals were built by early

Christians to provide care during times of plague based on the view that negligence that spread the disease further was murder. Historian Rodney Stark writes that there is much evidence suggesting in cities with Christian communities, the death rates due to plague may have been cut in half.

In 1527, when the bubonic plague reached Wittenberg, Germany, Martin Luther did not flee but remained to minister to the sick.[105] Tragically, his daughter Elizabeth died from the disease. Luther published a tract entitled, "Whether Christians Should Flee the Plague." In it, he writes,

> We die at our posts. Christian doctors cannot abandon their hospitals. Christian governors cannot flee their districts. Christian pastors cannot abandon their congregations. The plague does not dissolve our duties: It turns them to crosses, on which we must be prepared to die.

Stone suggests that in times of crisis we can be eager to sacrifice for others, even bearing costs to do so. We can follow health protocols to minimize our chance of infecting others. And we can protect our lifeline to a meaningful spiritual community that cares for our mind and soul.

In Comfort

But crises may not be our greatest spiritual challenge; comfort may be. One of the paradoxes of contemporary American life is that even as our existence has gotten more comfortable, on average, happiness has fallen.[106] Arthur Brooks reports that, according to the U.S. Census Bureau, average household income in the U.S., after adjusting for inflation, for each income quartile, was higher in 2019 than has ever been recorded. From 2000 to 2019, inflation-adjusted federal spending on education, training, employment, and social services increased by about 30 percent. From 1973 to 2016, the size of a new American home grew by about 1,000 square feet. Living space per person, on average, doubled. From 2000 to 2019, the percentage of Americans using the internet grew from 52% to 90%.

On the surface, that all sounds good. But despite these advances, average happiness in the U.S. is decreasing. The General Social Survey, which has measured social trends among Americans since 1972, shows a long-term, gradual decline in happiness from 1988 to 2020.

Especially to Christians, there may be nothing new about the idea that consumption does not lead to happiness. Brooks writes "consumerocracy, bureaucracy, and technocracy promise us greater satisfaction, but don't deliver. We don't get happier as our society gets richer, because we chase the wrong things."

But Christians are not immune to the pressures of our culture. Brooks advises that we limit consumption because after a certain lifestyle level, it does not bring happiness and that we not put faith in political leaders. But most importantly, he writes "don't trade love for anything".

Brooks refers to a study that followed the lives of hundreds of men who graduated from Harvard between 1939 and 1944 well into their 90s. The researchers wanted to know who flourished, who did not, and which decisions contributed to their sense of well-being. George Vaillant, a psychiatrist, was the lead researcher on the project for many years. In his book *Triumphs of Experience* he summarized the results this way: "Happiness is love. Full stop."[107]

The current director of the study, psychiatrist Robert Waldinger, filled in the details.[108] The subjects who were most depressed and lonely late in life—not to mention more likely to suffer from dementia, alcoholism, or other health problems—had neglected their close relationships. And the subjects who reported having the happiest lives were those with strong family ties, close friendships, and rich romantic lives.[109]

For all its promised benefits, prosperity may blind us to timeless sources of happiness: faith, family, friends, and meaningful work. Our culture encourages us to love things and use people. But that is backward. Now even research suggests, to be happy, use things and love people.

In Competition

Love is powerful, not just in times of crisis, or to navigate the perils of affluence, but when we compete.

Most of us know the power of clear goals and a compelling purpose; however, we do well to remember they are different things. Goals might be objectives we want to reach in the near future. But a purpose is bigger. Just ask Madeline DiRado.[110] At the age of 23, DiRado was something of a late bloomer when she qualified for the 2016 Olympics in swimming. She had barely missed qualifying for the 2012 Olympics. Everyone knew this would be her only chance to compete in an Olympic Games. She would swim in the 200-meter medley, 400-meter medley, 4x200-meter freestyle relay, and the 200-meter backstroke.

While swimming in the Olympics was her goal, it was not her purpose. She said, "I don't think God really cares about my swimming very much. This is not my end purpose, to make the Olympic team." When asked what she thinks God does care about DiRado replied,

> I think God cares about my soul and whether I'm bringing his love and mercy into the world. Can I be a loving, supportive teammate, and can I bless others around me in the same way God has been so generous with me?

In case you are wondering about those goals: DiRado medaled in all four events, taking home one bronze, one silver, and two gold medals. But those were just goals. They came and went. Her purpose endures.

You and I may have many goals. But what

is your purpose? Given the divisiveness of the culture surrounding us, and the unity in diversity of the Triune God sustaining us, what underlying motivation will guide the coming years and decades of your life?

Before going any further, would you pause and reflect on the following questions by writing in a journal or sharing your thoughts with a loved one?

Reflection Questions And Next Steps:

1. In your own words, how would you describe the way the members of the Trinity love One Another?
2. In a spoken or journaled prayer, ask the members of the Trinity to speak to your heart about the extent and strength of their love for you. Take time to listen.
3. Read John 13:34-35. What is your working definition of love?
4. How does the culture around you define love? Based on what you are seeing in the Trinity, how would you evaluate those definitions?
5. Who is the most loving person you know? Which relationship around you seems the most loving? What can you learn from their example?
6. How could you prepare now, so the next time

you face a crisis, you might respond in love?

7. What impact does your comfort have on your willingness to respond to others in love?
8. Even while competing, how might you retain the purpose of loving those around you?
9. If you were to take one creative, division-spanning step of love this week, what would it be? Will you give it a try?

Members Belonging to One Another

"For just as each of us has one body with many members, and these members do not all have the same function, so in Christ we, though many, form one body, and each member belongs to all the others."

ROMANS 12:4-5

Ron Bryce is a physician who describes the unforgettable experience during surgery of turning a patient's beating heart to provide another physician a better angle from which to work.[111] Despite this turning, the patient's heart continued to beat as billions of tiny heart cells communicated and coordinated their activities. Reading this account, I learned cells in the human heart rhythmically contract in unity, together producing a steady heartbeat. Separated from the heart in a test tube, these living cells will instinctively continue to beat, but not in coordination with one another. However, if the cells are brought back in contact with one another, writes Bryce, the instant they touch, their contractions again become synchronized.

That is the nature of heart cells. In isolation, they cannot accomplish their function no matter how hard they try. They were designed to be one of many cells within one heart. They have a unique function in the body, but they are not useful if they don't communicate and coordinate their efforts. Each heart cell needs other cells to fulfill its purpose. The only way a body can survive is through various members working together. All living bodies depend on the communication and coordination of their members.

After eleven chapters describing the dynamics of salvation (Romans 1-11), Paul reminds us in Romans 12:4-8 that all Christians are joined in one body as members with different functions.[112] Believing the Good News about Jesus Christ has social implications: you are joined to others, and others are joined to you. Justification by grace alone, through faith alone, in Christ alone, does not leave people alone. It connects people to God's Spirit and to the body of Christ, which is the church. It is easy for us to see that human bodies are not one despite their members. Human bodies are one *because* of their members. A human body without diversity would cease to be. Similarly, the church is not one despite its diverse members but because of them. In place of ethnic, national, or other temporary grounds for human unity, Paul advances the image of believers as members of one body in Christ.[113] Only in Christ do they function as a body.[114] Different people with diverse backgrounds, interests, and gifts undertaking distinct activities in the life and ministry of the church glorifies God by reflecting a bit of the unity and diversity of the Trinity. Membership in the body of Christ assimilates us into something much grander than ourselves, yet without marring or collapsing our individual identity. If anything, being members of one another enriches our identity. This should not be lost on us when more Americans of different ethnicities, educational levels, and political perspectives see church involvement as optional, and themselves as "spiritual but not religious".[115]

Early in our marriage, Alyse and I moved to Guaymas, Sonora, México. Our first-born son was two months old. In the coming years, we would add two more sons. Over the next ten years, living at quite a distance from our extended family members, our family of five became a tight unit. Our identities and our relationships developed in unique ways. Now that our sons are grown and live outside the home, there is nothing quite like the feeling when they all come home. When we are all together again, we re-tell stories about the silly events of those early years. We describe once awkward or even painful experiences in ways that now make us laugh aloud. We have a common language, a shared perspective. We are members of one another.

Heather King is a commentator for National Public Radio (NPR) and a recovering alcoholic. After coming to faith in Christ, she reflected on her initial experience with the church.[116]

> "My first impulse was to think, My God, I don't want to get sober (or in the case of the church,

> worship) with THESE nutcases! (or boring people, or people with different politics, taste in music, food, books, or whatever)" she writes.

Of course, nothing dethrones our ego like worshipping with people we cannot hand pick. What humility can be found, she says, in discovering we have been thrown in with unpromising people, who are broken, misguided, wishy-washy, and out for themselves. "People who are ... us." She points out we don't come to church to be with people who are like us in the way we want them to be. She writes,

> We come because we have staked our souls on the fact that Christ is the Way, the Truth, and the Life, and the church is the best place, the only place, to be while we all struggle to figure out what that means. We come because we'd be hard pressed to say which is the bigger of the two scandals of God: that he loves us—or that he loves everyone else.

In Romans 15:7 Paul wrote, "Accept one another, then, just as Christ accepted you, in order to bring praise to God." Jesus Christ is the Son, sent by the Father and full of the Spirit. Believing the gospel and following Christ is not just an individual religious decision. It leads to the fulfillment of what it means to be human - in community. A person comes to be "in Christ", to adopt Paul's frequent phrase, and Christ comes to dwell in that person, through the Spirit. Because Christians are saved by the same Redeemer, indwelt by the same Spirit, and living for the glory of the same Father, how important it is that we accept one another!

For years, the mystery of floating fire ants baffled scientists. Placed in water, an individual fire ant, whose body is denser than water, will flounder, struggle, and sink. But when fire ants band together they form life rafts that help them survive the flash floods of the Brazilian rainforests. As a unified raft, they can travel for months before reaching land.

A *Los Angeles Times* article summarized new research unlocking the secret of this natural mystery.[117] After collecting a bunch of ants, scientists dropped them into containers of water. The ants quickly spread out and formed themselves into rafts. Each ant used its claws and the adhesive pads on its legs to grip others. One researcher said, "At first it just looks like a tangle of bodies and limbs everywhere, but the longer you look at the picture, the more you're able to distinguish between different body parts and see the connection." Then the insects use air pockets that form around their bodies to keep themselves afloat.

The research sheds light on how the deeply social insects act together: “almost as if they’re part of a superorganism,” scientists said. “Some people almost think of ants as a fluid neural network: The colony itself is performing collective computations, but each ant is unaware of all these options,” said Iain Couzin, a biologist not involved in the study. Fire ants are better off together. So are we.

In his book *The Pastor*, Eugene Peterson described his wife Jan's perspective on what it means to be a pastor's wife.[118] The description is apt for all Christians as we enter more fully into life as members of the body of Christ. Peterson's words here have been modified slightly, substituting "church member" for "pastor's wife".[119]

> Being a church member is a vocation, a way of life. It means participation in an intricate web of hospitality, living at the intersection of human need and God's grace, inhabiting a community where men and women who don't fit are welcomed, where neglected children are noticed, where the stories of Jesus are told, and people who have no stories find that they do have stories, stories that are part of the Jesus story. Being a church member places us strategically yet unobtrusively at a heavily trafficked intersection between heaven and earth.

Being a member of a church requires, and provides, experiences that cannot be found in a mere membership class, things like patience, love, and forgiveness. Being members of one another is a lifestyle.

Many of us work in teams - at home and work, at church and in our community. Almost invariably, when we form teams we tend to look for talent. We often think exceptional people are the key to team success. While any of us could list professional athletes who help their teams succeed and talented colleagues who make outsized contributions, new research by Roderick Swaab and others suggests there is a limit to the team benefit brought by top talent.[120] For the basketball teams and soccer teams they studied, top talent did predict team success, but only to a point. The basketball and soccer teams with the greatest proportion of elite athletes actually performed worse than teams with moderate proportions of top-level players. The key was teamwork. In many activities, success requires collaboration and cooperation towards goals that are simply beyond the capability of any one participant. Interestingly, extreme levels of talent did not have the same negative effect on baseball teams, which experts have argued involves much less interdependent play than soccer and basketball. All teams have to strike a balance between competition and cooperation. Maybe before breaking the bank, or breaking hearts, in search of talent, it would be wise to break new ground building teamwork.

Take time now to think through the following questions to explore how this applies to you. Journal your responses or discuss them with a loved one.

Reflection Questions And Next Steps:

1. In your own words, how would you describe the way the Father, Son, and Spirit belong to One Another?
2. How integrated are the diverse members of your physical body?

3. Describe a time you felt excluded from others. What emotions did you feel?
4. Read Romans 15:7. Describe what you know about how Christ has accepted you.
5. Describe a time that people you respected accepted you. What emotions did you feel?
6. What spiritual practices might help you express the desire of God's indwelling Spirit that Christ-followers accept one another?
7. Read Ephesians 4:25. How can remembering we are members of one another lessen our tendency to self-deception?
8. Describe a positive experience on a sports team, community team, or work team. What made it so positive?
9. Think of a team on which you currently serve. What impact do you have on its teamwork?
10. This week, in one of your social circles, what would it look like for you to accept others intentionally, just as Christ has accepted you, in order to bring praise to God?

Demonstrating Kindness To One Another

"Be kind and compassionate to one another, forgiving each other, just as in Christ God forgave you."

EPHESIANS 4:32

"Be pitiful [kind], for every man [and woman] is fighting a hard battle."

JOHN WATSON (PEN NAME, IAN MACLAREN) (1850-1907)

Ever done a garage rescue? I do one or two per year. Perhaps you call them garage clean-up days. In our family, they happen when we can barely recognize our garage - let alone walk through it. Inevitably, it involves throwing things away. And that is followed by a sense of freedom and the space for life to continue.

Paul reminds us of other things we need to throw away. Some of them can do real damage. In Ephesians 4 he directs us, because we are members of one body, to "put off falsehood" (Ephesians 4:25). If we get angry, we are not to sin (Ephesians 4:26). We are to discipline ourselves away from unwholesome talk (Ephesians 4:29) and to "get rid of all bitterness, rage, and anger, brawling and slander, along with every form of malice" (Ephesians 4:31). The first-century church was an interesting place!

We are to throw out these vices, and the attitudes that fuel them, in part to make room for virtues that contribute to the development of individuals and the building of harmonious community. No matter what we have experienced, Paul commands us to "be kind and compassionate to one another, forgiving one another, just as in Christ God forgave you" (Ephesians 4:32). Paul can issue these commands because in Christ, God demonstrates that he is kind (Ephesians 2:7), compassionate (Mark 1:41), and graciously forgiving (Romans 8:32).

In Ephesians 4:32, behind the English word "kind" we find a Greek word *chrestos*, referring to what is useful. As opposed to things that are hard, harsh, sharp, or bitter, it describes things that are good, virtuous, and pleasant. Elsewhere the term describes the character of God (Luke 6:35) and the character of God's people (1 Corinthians 15:33).[121]

Eugene Peterson points out that while kindness or pity may be one of the most noble human emotions - self-pity may be among the most ignoble.[122] Pity is the capacity to enter into the pain of another person in order to act. But self-pity is an incapacity, a crippling emotional affliction that subtly distorts the very way we perceive reality. Pity discovers in others a need for love and healing and then fashions speech and action to bring strength. Self-pity, on the other hand, reduces life experiences to a series of personal wounds displayed to compel others' attention. Pity motivates mercy. Self-pity demotivates, leaving its host inert. Yet, if we respond in God-guided ways, pain can actually make us more kind. Pastor Ben Harden points out that if our own heart hasn't been broken, we may tend to be insensitive, except to those people we already like.[123]

Perhaps a test of true kindness is how we treat people we do not know. When Hunter Shamatt lost his wallet, he had little hope of getting it back, certainly not with interest.[124] But he did. When traveling to his sister's wedding, Hunter left his wallet on the airplane. It held the 20-year-old's identification card and debit card, as well as $60 and a signed paycheck. Hunter feared "the worst, that everything was gone," his mother Jeannie Shamatt wrote.

Fortunately, the man who found the wallet, Todd Brown, believed in kindness. He mailed everything back, and then some. Brown included a note that read:

> Hunter, found this on a Frontier flight from Omaha to Denver—wedged between the seat and wall. Thought you might want it back. All the best ... PS. I rounded your cash up to an even $100 so you could celebrate getting your wallet back. Have fun!!!

While others may have taken the cash, Brown added some. "I saw he was just a kid, 20 years old, he had a paycheck in there, so I figured, 'Well, he's doing his best to make ends meet.' I was 20 once," Brown said. In light of our current cultural divides, extending kindness to people we do not know is a particularly helpful act any of us could do.

Another test of kindness may be how we treat the people with whom we work. In 1938, the Whiting-Turner Contracting Company hired Willard Harriman as a timekeeper.[125] Harriman would serve at Whiting-Turner until 2014, some 75 years. In 1955, he became its second president. Under his leadership, Whiting-Turner grew from a Baltimore-area firm with $3.5 million in revenue to a national construction firm with $5 billion in revenue.

The company held its first corporate conference in the early 1990s. The national economy was emerging from a recession and the company was beginning to grow rapidly. As the meeting described how well Whiting-Turner had done in the last year, the tone of the meeting became boastful. Now Harriman had a firm set of values. In addition, he did not like meetings that lasted more than twenty minutes. This particular meeting had gone more than an hour-and-a-half. And, after all, he was the president of the company. So he raised his hand and asked, "Can I make a statement?" Harriman made his way to the platform and then walked to the newly vacant podium. He held it and looked into the eyes of the people making up the company. The room grew still and he said, "I want you to remember one thing. It's very, very, very, very, very, very, very important: be a nice person." And he walked off the platform.

One of the event organizers said, "I was part of the team that put that together. I don't remember a graph, a chart, a thing that I did, said or anybody else, but I never forgot that." In the seven years after Harriman's passing, Whiting-Turner nearly doubled in size. Whiting-Turner's success in those years did not come despite Harriman's kindness, but because of it.

Compassion is a cousin to kindness. In Ephesians 4:31, behind "compassionate" we find *eusplanchnos*, which can mean good-hearted, tenderhearted, or having inner emotions of affection.[126] The adjective is used in the New Testament only here and in 1 Peter 3:8, "Finally, all of you, be like-minded, be sympathetic, love one another, be compassionate and humble." It means to "show how your heart feels toward others" or "let your heart go out to others" or "feel sorrow in your heart for others".[127]

Somewhat famously, John 11:35 is the shortest verse in the Bible. Upon learning of the death of Lazarus, and seeing the grief of others, "Jesus wept." Jesus had close earthly relationships. He felt emotions and felt them deeply.

Jacques Monod was a French geneticist and Nobel Prize winner. In the course of a television program in Toronto with Mother Teresa, Monod shared his opinion that our entire destiny is locked up in our genes, which shape and direct our character and outlook, thus destroying the individual. As he held forth, Mother Teresa sat with her eyes closed and her hands folded, praying. When the program's host asked whether she had anything to say, she replied, "I believe in love and compassion," and resumed her devotions.[128] Compassion may be hard to measure objectively, but when we or someone we love experiences great need, receiving compassion can be overwhelming.

Much in Western culture prizes youth. Even so, certain advantages can come with age. Pastor William Buursma shared that as we get older, we can minister better under extreme circumstances because over the years we ourselves have suffered loss.[129] Compassion then, like kindness, may be a faculty that can grow over our lifetimes.

Nikolai Berdyaev (1874-1948) was a Russian political and Christian philosopher. Descended from an aristocratic and military family, Berdyaev criticized totalitarianism and the domination of the state over the individual. He was arrested and exiled because of his writing. Yet he retained his compassion:

> The question of bread for myself is a material question, but the question of bread for my neighbours, for everybody, is a spiritual and religious question ... Christians ought to be permeated with a sense of the religious importance of the elementary daily needs of people, the vast masses of

> people, and not to despise these needs from a sense of exalted spirituality.[130]

In Ephesians 4:31, behind “forgiving” we have a Greek word *charizomai*, meaning to show favor or to forgive because of one’s gracious attitude toward an individual.[131] A man in conversation with John Wesley once told him, "I never forgive." Wesley thought for a moment and then wisely replied, "Then, sir, I hope that you never sin."

Clara Barton founded the American Red Cross. The story is told that, reminded of a vicious deed someone had done to her years before, Clara acted as if she had never heard of the incident. "Don't you remember it?" her friend asked. "No," came Barton's reply. "I distinctly remember forgetting it." The intense friction and rapid fragmentation occurring in our culture mean forgiveness is something we would do well to practice now and in the future.

Clara Barton’s intentionality is impressive and often called for, but sometimes God calls us not to forget but to remember. Steve Hartman tells a story set in a small apartment building in North Minneapolis, where Mary Johnson, a 59-year-old teacher's aide, has not forgotten a vicious deed done to her.[132] In February 1993, Mary's son, Laramiun Byrd, was shot to death during an argument. He was 20 years old, and Mary's only child. The killer was 16-year-old Oshea Israel.

Mary wanted justice. Oshea was tried as an

adult and sentenced to 25 and a half years. He served 17 years before being released. Then he moved back to the neighborhood - right next door to Mary.

How a convicted murderer ended up living a doorjamb away from his victim's mother is a story, not of horrible misfortune - but of remarkable kindness. While he was serving time, Mary asked if she could meet Oshea in prison. As a devout follower of Christ, she felt compelled to see if there was some way, if somehow, she could forgive her son's killer.

During their first meeting, Mary told Oshea, "Look, you don't know me. I don't know you. Let's just start with right now." Oshea says, "And I was befuddled myself."

They met regularly. When he got out, Mary introduced Oshea to her landlord - who with Mary's blessing, invited Oshea to move into the building. Today they don't just live close - they are close.

Mary was able to forgive. She credits God with giving her the strength - but also concedes a selfish motive. “Unforgiveness is like cancer,” Mary says. “It will eat you from the inside out. It's not about that other person, me forgiving him does not diminish what he's done. Yes, he murdered my son - but the forgiveness is for me. It's for me.”

For Oshea, it hasn't been that easy. “I haven't totally forgiven myself yet, I'm learning to forgive myself. And I'm still growing toward trying to forgive myself.” To that end, Oshea has gotten busy working at a recycling plant by day and attending college by night. He says he's determined to pay back Mary's compassion by contributing to society. He's already working on it - singing the praises of God and forgiveness at prisons and churches. Oshea says, "A conversation can take you a long way."

Paul's statement in Ephesians 4:32 follows a certain logic: what God has done in Christ for believers, the theme of the first half of Ephesians, provides the norm and the grounds for the behavior of believers.[133] God's forgiveness of believers becomes the paradigm and the fuel for believers to forgive one another.

Would you take time to pray and reflect on these questions and next steps? How does this connect with your life? Use a journal or share with a loved one.

Reflection Questions And Next Steps:

1. Take a moment to reflect on the kindness the Triune persons experience from One Another. How do you conceive it?
2. How would you describe the kindness the Trinity has extended to you? What spiritual practices might increase your awareness of

this kindness throughout a typical day?

3. Read Ephesians 4:26-32. At this time in your life, is there anything you need to “put off”?
4. What hinders you from expressing kindness to others?
5. What helps you express kindness?
6. Describe a time someone surprised you with kindness.
7. What unwanted pain in your past or present may God want to use to build compassion in you?
8. What speaks to you from the Mary Johnson-Oshea Israel story?
9. Whom do you need to forgive, whether or not they ask for forgiveness, simply because Jesus has forgiven you?
10. Whom do you need to ask for forgiveness? When will you do it?

Encouraging One Another

"Encourage one another and build each other up, just as in fact you are doing."

1 THESSALONIANS 5:11

It started with a folder. Then it grew to two folders. Then I went to a box. Now I have boxes of encouragement notes written by people in churches I have served.

Words of affirmation strengthen me. It is good to have these notes. Sometimes it is *necessary* to have them. Life can be tough. Ministry can be tough. Leading is tough. Not everything works. Plans don't materialize. Disappointment happens. Doubt enters. Discouragement comes. Finding encouragement, again and again, is vital. On occasion, I read some of those notes and remember sweet moments of ministry leadership. Other times, during the hustle and bustle of a busy season, I simply remember these notes exist, evidence of God's goodness in ministry.

Words are powerful. *Your* words are powerful. Our words influence others - and they influence us. Just ask Darren Young. A Hawaii judge sentenced him to write 144 nice things about his ex-girlfriend.[134] He reportedly sent her dozens of offensive messages, which violated a protection order. Then Judge Rhonda Loo told Young he must come up with new praises to give to his former girlfriend. "For every nasty thing you said about her, you're going to say a nice thing. No repeating words," the Judge said. That is court-ordered encouragement. How wonderful we have God's Spirit in us to help provide words of encouragement for others.

People around you may need encouragement more than we think. A CDC report indicates the coronavirus pandemic is associated with an increase in mental health difficulties because of the morbidity of the disease and challenges related to social distancing and stay-at-home orders.[135] Nearly 41% of all respondents reported at least one adverse mental or behavioral health condition. And 31% said they had experienced symptoms of anxiety or depression in the 30 days before taking the survey.

However, the pandemic appears to have had a particularly detrimental effect on young people. Among people 18-24 years old, 75% reported having at least one adverse mental or behavioral health symptom, making them by far the most impacted demographic. Of this group, 63% reported symptoms of anxiety or depression. Fully 25% reported using substances to cope with pandemic-related stress or emotions. And significantly, 25.5% of young people said they had seriously considered suicide within 30 days of taking the survey. Words and acts of encouragement alone will not solve each of these complex challenges, but they can help anyone feel more loved, listened to, and hopeful.

In the first century, when the Thessalonian Christians endured persecution, Paul, Silas, and Timothy wanted to encourage their readers. They reminded them the day of Jesus' return was approaching. They called their readers to "be sober, putting on faith and love as a breastplate, and the hope of salvation as a helmet" (1 Thessalonians 5:8). After all, God did not appoint them to suffer wrath, "but to receive salvation through our Lord Jesus Christ" (1 Thessalonians 5:9). "Therefore," they remind, "encourage one another and build each other up, just as in fact you are doing" (1 Thessalonians 5:11).

The hope of Christ's return is not an excuse for idleness, but an incentive to help one another grow spiritually.[136] "Every church member has a duty to help in "building up" the community, so that it may attain spiritual maturity," writes F. F. Bruce. This describes not an event, but a process, not an incident, but a lifestyle. Early churches wisely included opportunities for believers to build one another up. Believers may not always need to hear something new, but we often need to be reminded of what we already know, as Paul's ministry demonstrates.

Behind "encouragement" in Thessalonians 5:11, we find the Greek word *parakaleo*, which means "to call to one's side."[137] Barnabas was a compelling New Testament encourager who called Paul to his side to encourage him.[138] Born in Cyprus and given the name Joseph, he may have been one of many Jews who migrated to Jerusalem where he became an early convert to Christianity. He sold a field shortly afterward and gave the money to the Jerusalem church. "Barnabas" was a nickname given by the apostles meaning "Son of Encouragement" (Acts 4:36-37).

Unlike most Christians at the time, Barnabas believed Paul's conversion story, and he smoothed the way for the Jerusalem church to accept the former persecutor. Barnabas then went on to pastor the growing church in Antioch, while Paul returned to Tarsus. Barnabas later invited Paul to come and co-pastor with him in Antioch. In 48 AD, Barnabas set off with his cousin Mark and Paul to evangelize cities in Asia Minor. Though Mark deserted the party early on, Barnabas and Paul preached, performed miracles, and endured persecution together. How grateful we can be that Barnabas encouraged Paul early in Paul's ministry.

Have you ever had a Barnabas in your life? I sure have.

Early in our ministry, I had been working hard but I felt discouraged. Many days our project seemed too big and too hard. In quiet, rational moments, the glimmers of hope we experienced seemed just too few and far between to believe this would actually work. So I poured out my frustration, disappointment, and discouragement to a friend a generation older who had done similar work. She listened and listened and then in her inimitable way looked into my eyes and said, "It is hard. But if anyone can do it, it is you." Those words put steel in my spine. She knew how hard this was; she had been there. And she still thought it could happen. I left that conversation encouraged. Our circumstances had not changed, but I had. Her encouragement gave me new resolve to see things through.

Sometimes we are called to encourage a total stranger - and end up inspiring someone looking on. An unidentified man on a Southwest Airlines flight was identified as a "flight angel" for comforting a 96-year old woman he did not know who was flying for the first time in 15 years.[139] Nearby passenger Megan Ashley, posted photos of the pair on Facebook, and explained that the woman was going to Kansas City to visit her family for her birthday, but was "scared of flying."

Ashley said,

> She asked for this man's hand during takeoff and then hugged him again when experiencing turbulence. This gentleman gladly took her hand, let her hold onto him, calmed her by talking to her, and explaining everything that was happening. He was simply there for her. He knew just what to do the entire flight to help.

She also said that the man went above and beyond even after the flight. He held her bag and helped her get off the plane and into the wheelchair. When she got confused wondering where her daughter went (whom she called "her sister"), he stayed with her until she caught up with her daughter.

Ashley said she walked away from the flight "sobbing happy tears" at the man's selflessness. She wrote in the caption, "Hats off to you sir, for your kind heart and your compassion toward someone whom you've never met." We often underestimate the encouragement our actions can bring others.

We sometimes think talented people do not need encouragement. In light of their abilities, contributions, and contracts we can forget that they experience difficulties as much as if not more than others. And they can be impacted by words, just like anyone else. NBA star Paul George is one example. After a decisive win in their 2020 playoff series against the Dallas Mavericks, the LA Clippers star was candid and vulnerable in his postgame interview. He implied that his poor shooting in the three previous games was due to his struggle with depression and anxiety.[140]

George later explained, "It was just a little bit of everything. I underestimated mental health, honestly. I had anxiety. A little bit of depression. Just being locked in here. I just wasn't there. I checked out." George referred to the tightly-regulated confines of the Disney World "bubble." To prevent any positive tests for the coronavirus, the NBA gathered its playoff teams inside the Disney facilities, with players housed and games played onsite. George continued, "Shout-out to the people that were in my corner, that gave me words. They helped big time, help get me right, [get] me back in great spirits. I can't thank them enough."

The Clippers head coach at the time, Doc Rivers, said, “This is not a normal environment, OK? It just isn't. [George] and I sat in my room after the game. We just had a long talk, not all about basketball, really. Several players did it. Guys were knocking on his door." Teammate Montrezl Harrell confirms this, admitting he understood the challenge of maintaining emotional equilibrium after having grieved the loss of his grandmother. Harrell said of George, "We just wanted to get him out of that. Get him out of his room ... just constantly be around him to show him that we're here with him.” George said he felt the difference the morning of that game. “I mean, I just felt it. My energy, my spirit was changed. That's all it needed.”

In 1 Thessalonians 5:11, “build each other up” relies on *oikodomeo*, a Greek word meaning to build a house.[141] You and I may not have the skills necessary to build a house, but each of us, every day, can build the environment we call home.

On May 24, 1965, a thirteen-and-a-half-foot boat quietly slipped out of the marina at Falmouth, Massachusetts.[142] Its destination? England. It would be the smallest craft ever to make the voyage. Its name? Tinkerbelle. Its pilot? Robert Manry, a copy editor for the Cleveland Plain Dealer, who felt ten years at the desk was more than enough, so he took a leave of absence to fulfill his secret dream.

Manry was afraid, not of the ocean, but of all those people who would try to talk him out of the trip. So he didn't share it with many, just some relatives and especially his wife, Virginia. She was his greatest source of support.

The trip was anything but pleasant. He spent sleepless nights trying to cross shipping lanes without getting run down and sunk. Weeks at sea caused his food to become tasteless. Loneliness, that age-old monster of the deep, led to terrifying hallucinations. His rudder broke three times. Storms swept him overboard. Had it not been for the rope knotted around his waist, he would never have been able to pull himself back on board. Finally, after seventy-eight days alone at sea, he sailed into Falmouth, England.

During those nights at the tiller, he had fantasized about what he would do once he arrived. He expected to check into a hotel, eat dinner alone, then the next morning see if, perhaps, the Associated Press might be interested in his story.

But word of his approach had spread. To his amazement, three hundred vessels, with horns blasting, escorted Tinkerbelle into port. Forty thousand people stood screaming and cheering him to shore. Robert Manry, a copy editor with a dream and perseverance, became an overnight hero.

His story has been told around the world. But Robert couldn't have done it alone. Standing on the dock was another hero: Virginia. Refusing to be rigid or negative when Robert's dream was taking shape, she allowed him the freedom to pursue it.

Dreamers and daredevils like Robert Manry are less born than made. The environment in which we live has much to do with whether our dreams flounder or flourish. Certainly, our world needs more risk-takers like Robert Manry, but how desperately our homes need encouragers like Virginia.

Virginia reminds us of the power of our response to a new idea. Pastor Andy Stanley says that because we are realists, when someone shares a new idea, it is tempting to ask a "How" question: "How will you pay for that?" "How will you have time for that?"[143] We don't realize those worthwhile questions are meant for later. Visionaries and innovators rarely have it all worked out at the beginning. We can make it a habit first, to say "Wow!" "Wow, that is so creative!" "Wow, that is something new!" "Wow, I would love to see that!" To give room for creativity and innovation to blossom, before we ask "*How?*" we would be wise to exclaim "*Wow!*"

If you want to be the kind of person who can readily encourage others, one place to start is your Bible. According to a new study conducted during the pandemic, a contentious election, and a time of social unrest, the American Bible Society, with assistance from Harvard University's Human Flourishing Program, found a strong correlation between Scripture reading and hope.[144]

Frequent Bible readers rated themselves 33 points more hopeful than irregular Scripture readers did in two surveys of more than 1,000 people done six months apart. The study also found that people are more hopeful when they read Scripture more frequently.

On a scale of 1 to 100, with 100 being the most hopeful, Americans who reported reading the Bible three or four times per year scored 42; people who read monthly scored 59; weekly readers scored, 66; and people reading the Bible multiple times per week scored 75.

Bible reading—along with other forms of community and discipleship, such as going to church or participating in a small group—appear to contribute to a sense of well-being and happiness, said Tyler VanderWeele, director of Harvard's Human Flourishing Program. "The churches have an important and profound role in contributing to people's well-being in general," he said.

Paul's exhortation carries the idea of undertaking a process to increase the potential or strength of someone else.[145] Sometimes it is our example in facing hardship that encourages others. And sometimes that example is passed on to another generation.

Joshua Haldeman grew up on the prairies of Saskatchewan. When the Great Depression hit Canada, Haldeman lost his five-thousand-acre farm and had to start over from scratch. He tried his hand at chiropractic medicine and politics. Then Haldeman discovered his passion—flying airplanes.[146]

In 1950, Haldeman uprooted his family and moved halfway around the world to South Africa, even though he had never been there before. With the help of his wife, Winnifred, and their children, he disassembled his 1948 single-engine airplane. The airplane was packed into crates and shipped to South Africa. Once it arrived, his family reassembled it.

A few years later, Joshua and Winnifred Haldeman embarked on a grueling flight from Africa to Australia - and back. They are believed to be the only private pilots to have ever made that flight in a single-engine airplane.[147]

Few people have heard of Joshua and Winnifred Haldeman, but you've probably heard of their grandson, Elon Musk. Musk's entrepreneurial exploits are well documented. He has turned the automotive and aerospace industries upside down. At SpaceX headquarters, there are two giant posters of Mars. One shows a cold, barren planet. The other looks a lot like Earth. The second poster represents Musk's life purpose—colonizing Mars.

In real life - not science fiction - how does one even conceive of colonizing a planet? Dreams are not conceived and dreamers do not develop in a vacuum. One of Musk's biographers noted, "Throughout his childhood, Elon heard many stories about his grandfather's exploits and sat through countless slide shows that documented his travels." Those stories were the seedbed of Musk's imagination. Those stories are the shoulders he stands on.

It is a wonderful blessing to have that kind of innovation and drive in your family tree, but none of us choose our families. We can, however, choose our friends. Long after their deaths, many still enjoy the imaginative writing of C. S. Lewis and J. R. R. Tolkien. Their creative and theological genius was stimulated by weekly meetings with the "Inklings", a gathering of thinkers and friends who met to critique one another's writing and to discuss current events and life in general.[148]

The Inklings heard and discussed drafts of Tolkien's *Lord of the Rings*, Lewis's *The Great Divorce*, and others' work. Lively discussions ensued on education, pain, and who was the most important man in various countries. Disagreements broke out and members sometimes expressed intense dislike for each other's work. But they hung together and kept at it. The Inklings began meeting in Lewis's rooms at Magdalen College at Oxford on Thursday nights in 1933 and continued the tradition until 1950. Tuesday morning gatherings at the Eagle and Child pub (also known as the Bird and Baby) continued until Lewis's death.

What insights were shared in those regular meetings, what encouragement to continue their writing, we may never know. But the literary world is better for it. How does your choice of friends hinder or help your work? To whose work could you bring the right nudge to help it reach its potential?

We often think of encouragement as helpful acts we give or receive or welcome phrases we speak or hear. Recent research suggests, however, that those adopting the positive, encouraging outlook from which such acts come, may not only do good but may live longer.[149] The study found that women who characterize themselves as having the highest levels of optimism live 15% longer than the least optimistic women and have a 50% greater chance of reaching age 85. The most optimistic men live 11% longer and are 70% more likely to reach 85.

One key seems to involve the body's stress response. Studies have shown that chronic stress can lead to inflammation, which can cause many diseases. Compared to pessimists, the most optimistic people say they sleep better and longer, are less likely to be sleepy during the day, and are 74% more likely to report no symptoms of insomnia.

Lead author Rosalba Hernandez, a professor at the University of Illinois, says: "Optimists are more likely to engage in active problem solving and to interpret stressful events in more positive ways." People who are optimistic and goal-oriented agree strongly with statements like "I can find something positive, even in the worst situations." Optimists experience reductions in depression, anxiety, and panic disorders. Looking on the bright side, apart from being more fun, may just help you live longer.

At this point, spend time praying and reflecting on the role of encouragement in your life. Think about ways you receive it and ways you give it. Then share responses to these prompts in your journal or with a loved one.

Reflection Questions And Next Steps:

1. Today, how would you describe your level of encouragement?
2. Ask the Trinity to remind you of specific ways they have encouraged you.
3. Ask the Trinity for inspiration about how you could encourage someone in your social circle. Jot down and think through anything you sense the Trinity would have you do.
4. Which relationships in your life tend to enhance you -- and which tend to leave you feeling diminished?
5. Describe someone you know who is encouraging.
6. How might creating, stocking, and occasionally reviewing an Encouragement Folder help you?
7. Read 1 Thessalonians 5:11.
8. How would you rate the culture of encouragement in your home? This week, what words or actions could you deploy to take it

up a notch?

9. How would you rate the level of anxiety or depression of one person living close to you? What is one thing you might do this week to bring encouragement?
10. The next time they share an idea, to what dreamer, creative or innovator could you delay asking "How?" and simply say "*Wow!*"?
11. When it comes to the words and images of your social media posts, have you made up your mind not to put any stumbling block or obstacle in the way of a brother or sister (Romans 14:13b)?
12. Optimists may live longer. When you reflect on the love of the Triune God for you, as you go through life, what mental outlook will you adopt?

Serving One Another

"Offer hospitality to one another without grumbling. Each of you should use whatever gift you have received to serve others, as faithful stewards of God's grace in its various forms."

1 PETER 4:9-10

"The greatest among you will be your servant."

JESUS, MATTHEW 23:11

"I don't know what your destiny will be, but one thing I do know: the only ones among you who will be really happy are those who have sought and found how to serve."

ALBERT SCHWEITZER (1875-1965), MISSIONARY PHYSICIAN, ORGANIST, AND WRITER

In the ancient world, hospitality was important, but it was doubly so for Christians.[150] Christian missionaries traveled from place to place without anything like the safety and convenience of today's hotels and restaurants. They relied on local Christian residents for food and lodging. Christians often went without the support of non-Christian relatives and friends and so looked to their fellow Christians to help meet some basic needs. Also, churches did not have their own buildings at the time of Peter's writing, or long thereafter, so Christian homes were used for worship (see, for example, Romans 16:5, 1 Corinthians 16:19, Colossians 4:15). Far from a form of entertainment, self-promotion, or indulgence, hospitality among Christians in the first century was often a means of survival.

Hospitality is a concrete expression of mutual love among Christians and therefore best understood as a responsibility of each member of the church, not something determined by having one or another gift (*charisma*).[151] Hospitality provides the context and attitude in which Christian ministries can operate. *Philoxenos* is the Greek word behind "hospitable" in 1 Peter 4:9. It means a lover of foreigners.[152] How do you feel about foreigners? How do you feel about people whose ideas might seem foreign to you?

Hospitality may not sound like much, but it is. It's a virtue that regularly punches above its weight. Consider the case of Marcella, born into a noble Roman family in 325 AD.[153] Although widowed at an early age, and childless, she decided to not remarry, instead devoting herself to serving Christ and the church. She led Bible studies and prayer meetings among other noblewomen and founded the first convent for women in the Western church. She gave liberally to help other Christians, even offering her palace as a sanctuary for persecuted Christians. When the fourth-century scholar Jerome was commissioned to make a newly revised translation of the Gospels, he moved into Marcella's retreat house for the duration of the task. For three years, Jerome depended on Marcella and her guests to critique his ongoing work, which eventually became the Latin Vulgate Bible. Often we do not know the ultimate impact of our hospitality.

Today, how frequently one opens one's home to others varies by country. And this may offer Americans like me something to learn. According to a recent survey, Mexicans and Argentinians are the most frequent hosts, out of 17 countries surveyed, with 42% and 39%, respectively, entertaining guests at home daily or weekly.[154] They are followed by Brazilians at 36%, Italians at 34%, and Chinese at 30%. Among respondents from the U.S., 21% said they entertain guests at home once a week or more.

Crises can spur us to creative acts of hospitality. Pina Andelora and Angelo Picone are musicians accustomed to performing for passers-by on Spaccanapoli, the historic main street that traverses the center of Naples, Italy.[155] The virus disrupted their work and their means of contributing to the life of their city - or so they thought. When they realized the lockdown also prevented local soup kitchens from serving people who are homeless, they reinvigorated a tradition. They began preparing meals from their home for people in need but chose an ancient delivery system. Piccone said, “We relied on an old Neapolitan custom — lowering food baskets from our balcony.” They included in the basket a slogan from a legendary Neopolitan doctor known for treating the poor: “Those who can, put something in, those who can't, help yourself.” The baskets awakened a new level of generosity in the city. "People out shopping for groceries now stop by our baskets and leave something inside," says Piccone. "Pasta, sugar, coffee, and cans of tuna." Pictures and videos of homeless people receiving food from suspended baskets prompted people beyond Naples to contribute. Certainly, the form and distribution of hospitality can be wonderfully creative.

Tragedy, also, is an opportunity for powerful hospitality. One Sunday in Calabasas, California, The Church in the Canyon engaged in typical Sunday morning activities. The morning was shattered by the sound of a helicopter crashing into the hillside across the street. Pastor Bob Bjerkaas immediately led his congregation to pray. The pastor expected to see first responders. What he did not expect to see, that day and for many days, was a steady flow of news reporters, camera crews, and fans.[156] They came to remember retired basketball star Kobe Bryant, his daughter Gianna and seven other precious people who lost their lives in the crash.

Although completely unprepared, Pastor Bob and his church quickly found ways to provide hospitality. The church offered coffee, water, and fruit as refreshments. They opened the church's restrooms and provided power strips to charge phones. They engaged grieving visitors and invited them to pray. "The Bible says we're to practice hospitality," said Bjerkaas:[157]

> That's what we did. We prayed with people who were emotionally overwhelmed, in tears, and in open grief. Sometimes all people need is a hug, a 'God bless you,' a short prayer, and a cup of water. I've always believed more good is done in this life if you can get close to the ground and share life with the people around you.

Practicing hospitality, especially on short notice, is demanding. Perhaps this is why Peter adds that hospitality should be practiced without complaining, grumbling, or displeasure (*gongusmos*). In other words, we are to offer hospitality with gladness. Some things cannot be done quickly; hospitality is one of those things. Hospitality demands time, one of our most precious possessions. Thus, offering hospitality often requires an adjustment of our heart attitude. It turns out God is often involved in the details of our hospitality. G. K. Chesterton once quipped, "We make our friends; we make our enemies, but God makes our next door neighbor. We have to love our neighbor because he is there."[158]

I have benefitted from and witnessed tremendous hospitality. The summer after graduating from college, I lived with a local pastor in the rural town of Uspantán, in the Quiché Department (state), in Guatemala. His home had been damaged in an earthquake, and not completely repaired. Yet he and his wife remained there, ministering to me and to poor indigenous people who lived in the surrounding hills. Once a week my host put on a white coat and became their doctor, listening to them describe their ailments and delivering advice and sometimes medicine from his meager supply. During the week, he hiked the hills, visiting their homes, leading Bible studies, praying for families, and encouraging believers.

Healthy churches brim with hospitality. Before I married, I served at a church and lived with family after family. In another church I served, one family had cared for over 100 foster babies. And in another church, I met a grown man, who years earlier had been sent from Vietnam by his parents along with his siblings, on a makeshift boat. After escaping danger on land, they faced a harrowing journey on the open sea, including threats from pirates. They were rescued and later a U.S. family adopted them. That family raised these children and eventually helped their parents emigrate to the U.S. What impact can be brought from hospitality!

1 Peter 4:10 reminds us to "use whatever gift you have received to serve others." Underneath "gift" we find the Greek word charisma describing a gift

of grace or a gift with God as the donor.[159] As we would expect, this term is used in various New Testament contexts to describe ways God's Spirit endows believers for service. Our gifts can make mundane moments deeply meaningful, as renowned cellist Yo-Yo Ma recently illustrated.[160] Ma has a residence in Pittsfield, MA. After traveling to a local community college campus to receive his second vaccination shot, Ma gave something back. He had asked the clinic managers if he could perform a few songs for people waiting in the observation area. Wearing a mask and socially distanced, the 18-time Grammy award winner provided a brief, impromptu concert to the delight of those listening. One observer said, "Many people were moved to tears. It was an exceptional moment at the end of a long day of giving shots." For Ma, this was not entirely new. In the early days of the pandemic, he provided a series of live recordings aimed at comforting those forced to stay at home.[161] Of course, very few of us have the musical gifting and training of Yo-Yo Ma, but each of us can intentionally use the talents and resources we do have to bless others.

In 1 Peter 4:10 we read, "Each of you should ... serve others ..." Behind serve we find the verb *diakoneo* meaning "to be a servant or attendant, to serve, wait upon, minister."[162] Even in our divided culture, service is attractive. My wife Alyse is a servant. Before we became a couple, she and I gathered with a group of college-age friends for worship in a park. Backpacks, car keys, blankets, and shoes were strewn about the grass. My wallet and guitar case were in there somewhere too. While I played guitar and we sang, suddenly the park's high-pressure sprinklers came on shooting giant arcs of water at us and all around us. Everyone scattered, grabbing their personal items as best they could. Except for Alyse. She grabbed my wallet and guitar case to keep them dry. You can learn a lot about someone in a moment of surprise. Over the years, that same servant attitude has characterized her, surfacing in many acts of hospitality and influencing our family culture.

Yet ironically powerful trends in our culture advocate for just the opposite mentality. Particularly when counseling young people about their future, Americans are prone to say things like "follow your passion," "pursue your dreams," or "do what you love and love what you do." It is fair to ask: Do these assertions lead people to clarity, fulfillment, and flourishing? New evidence suggests they may not. A study by researchers from Stanford University and Yale-NUS College found that "following your passion" is likely to lead to overly limited pursuits, inflated career and financial expectations, and early or eventual burnout.[163] The study's authors concluded:

> People are often told to find their passion as though passions and interests are pre-formed and must simply be discovered. This idea, however, has hidden motivational implications ... Urging people to find their passion may lead them to put

all their eggs in one basket but then to drop that basket when it becomes difficult to carry.

While our culture tells us to "look within," assuming a fixed set of passions to guide us on our way, researchers found more positive results among those who allow room for interests and intelligence to develop over time. The study encourages us to ask: Are we still looking only to the self or are we looking outward and upward as well?

Commentator David Brooks would appreciate the question. He describes such phrases - including “chart your own course”, “march to the beat of your own drummer” and “find yourself”- as “the litany of expressive individualism, which is still the dominant note in American culture.”[164] But, he reminds,

> This mantra misleads on nearly every front ... Most successful young people don’t look inside and then plan a life. They look outside and find a problem, which summons their life ... Most people don’t form a self and then lead a life. They are called by a problem, and the self is constructed gradually by their calling ... The purpose in life is not to find yourself. It’s to lose yourself.

Against what our culture sometimes suggests, an orientation to serve can be effective, even at high levels of leadership. Cheryl Bachelder led a fruitful career in the consumer products industry serving at companies like Procter and Gamble, Gillette, and RJR Nabisco. Along the way, she put her career on hold several times to be a full-time mother and homemaker. In 2007, she was elected CEO of what is now known as Popeye's Louisiana Kitchen. A committed Christian in the workplace, Bachelder turned her company around with a focus on serving others.[165] She writes,

> The Bible verse that's on my calendar every day is Philippians 2:3. Because I haven't found one that's more paramount to how I want to lead in my family and in my work. And that is, "Do nothing from selfish ambition or conceit, but in humility count others more significant than yourselves." I really like the choice of words around counting others more significant than yourselves. I find that biblical perspective really challenging in every aspect of my day—how I'm spending my time, the decisions that I make. To put them through a filter of whether I'm thinking about myself or whether I'm thinking about others. Am I doing this because I'll get a bigger bonus check? Or am I really thinking about the long-term interest of this company? Am I doing this truly for my franchise owners, or am I getting some personal benefit that I haven't been willing to acknowledge? Those kinds of provocative self-mirror questions hold you to a higher standard. I always say servant leadership is an aspiration, because you can really never claim you've arrived. Because as soon as you do, someone will find you—and in a trap of self-interest. It's something you're always working to-

ward.

Before her arrival, Popeye's had cycled through four CEOs in seven years. Then, Bachelder led Popeye's through ten straight years of growth, and its stock price rose from $15 per share to $79 per share.

Some, like Bachelder, serve from the front. Others serve from behind.

Depending on your age, you may have encountered Batman first through one of the 18 Batman films produced between 1943 and 2022, in the weekly TV show that aired from 1966-1968, in reruns that ran long thereafter, or even through the comic book in which he debuted in 1939. However, no matter when you encountered Batman for the first time, you also encountered Alfred Pennyworth, Bruce Wayne's faithful butler, valet, friend, and father figure.

While Batman faces down evil enemies, he knows that back at Wayne Manor, a calm, resourceful, and trustworthy person is taking care of everything else: maintaining the Batmobile, building the batcomputer, and keeping the Caped Crusader's costume in top shape.[166] Alfred can remove bullets so Batman doesn't have to go to the hospital when injured. And, depending on which Batman you prefer, Alfred has single-handedly mastered computer programming, computer engineering, electrical engineering, chemical engineering, mechanical engineering, nanotechnology, and biotechnology. Yeah, he's good to have around. Alfred uses these skills, not for himself, but to advance Batman's cause. Alfred is not about self-realization but service.

The power of serving really comes home when we face a moment of need. My family and I did church planting work in México. One Sunday we looked forward to opening a remodeled wing of our church building. Months of planning and work had gone into this special Sunday. This day our new church would create a first impression in the mind of our visitors. Yet as I entered the building, immediately I knew something was wrong. A horrible smell permeated the room. We searched high and low and could not find anything wrong. Finally, not long before people would begin to arrive, we found a cat had died behind our building. In the desert heat, his decomposing body was creating quite a smell. (Sorry, cat lovers.) Something had to be done, and fast. One of our leaders looked at me and said, "Derek, don't worry. I'm your cat guy." Dressed in his Sunday best, he put garbage bags over each hand and scooped the cat's body into a third bag, which he tied and removed. Shortly, the smell went away. Our service went forward without distraction. How I came to treasure that brother in Christ! And I found a new level of appreciation for those willing to serve in undesirable tasks. Even today, our family uses the phrase "He's a cat guy" to honor those who stand out through service.

Who is serving you well, that you might have slowly started to take for granted? How might a renewed commitment to serve affect your life?

In 1 Peter 4, the word translated stewards is *oikonomos*. It describes "one who rules a house" where oikos is "a house," and nomos is "a law".[167] It can refer to one who has the authority and responsibility for something, an administrator or a manager.[168] In Galatians 4:2, the term denotes a superior servant responsible for housekeeping, the direction of other servants, and the care of young children.[169] A steward, in Greek culture at that time, was a slave who managed the household affairs of his master (compare Luke 12:42; 16:1–8). To be a steward of God's gifts means those endowments are not for the believer's enjoyment and benefit; they are given to enable her to serve her fellow believers better. "Stewards" is plural in our passage meaning all Christians are entrusted with this task.[170]

Tim Boyle isn't just the President and CEO at Columbia Sportswear, he is also its steward. A rival to outdoor brands like REI and North Face, Columbia Sportswear had to close all of its brick-and-mortar locations after the enactment of stay-at-home orders aimed at reducing the spread of the coronavirus. The company responded by invoking a "catastrophic pay program," which enabled its 3,500 employees to continue to receive pay during the indefinite closure. At the same time, Boyle sacrificed almost all of his salary. After earning $3 million in 2018, in 2020 he would receive only $10,000. In addition, 10 different upper-level executives volunteered to reduce their pay by fifteen percent. Boyle said: "Columbia has been in business since 1938 and has weathered many storms by keeping our focus on the well-being of consumers, employees, and the larger community."[171] Stewards do not put themselves first; they focus on the well-being of the people and assets entrusted to their care.

Skilled stewards play an outsized, but often underappreciated, role on teams. In his book *The Captain Class*, Sam Walker examines hidden forces that helped create the world's greatest sports teams.[172] One surprising finding relates to the make-up of great team captains: they took care of tough, unglamorous tasks. They were rarely stars. Often they did unseen work. Walker gives the following example:

> In 1962, when Brazil won its second consecutive World Cup, its team's unquestioned star was Pelé, arguably the greatest soccer player of all time. The prevailing view is that Pelé's brilliance, demonstrated by his 77 goals, was the team's driving force. But Pelé was never made captain—nor did he lobby for the job. The team's primary leader was Hilderaldo Bellini, a tough and humble central defender who, during a nine-year stint with Brazil, never scored a goal.
>
> Bellini was a functionary. He was not a star. While Pelé attended to the pressures of celebrity, Bellini took care of the daily, hourly grunt work of unifying the team. He cleaned up their mistakes with his fearless defense; often leaving the pitch bruised and bloodied, he calmly urged his teammates forward when their confidence sagged.

Walker concludes, "The captains on my list were rarely exceptional talents ... The leader's job wasn't to dazzle on the field but to labor in the shadows of the stars, to carry water for the team, to lead from the back."

What impact would there be on the people in your family, work team, or church group if you viewed yourself as a steward, responsible not just for your own well-being, but for the group's well-being?

And then, in 1 Peter 4:10, behind "various forms" we find the Greek term *poikilos* which modifies the term grace. It means particolored, variegated, diversified, or manifold.[173] Given the breadth of this term, have we misunderstood God's grace as too limited? Could God's grace to us be even more varied in its forms than we have assumed or expected?

Because of the dazzling nature of the grace we have received from the Triune God, no situation is beyond us stewarding that grace for the good of others. This can happen at any time and place, as a group of flight attendants and passengers on a Southwest Airlines flight point out.

When Dustin and Caren Moore asked a flight attendant for help changing their newborn daughter, they received more than they expected.[174] One of the flight attendants named Jenny asked the parents why they were flying with such a young baby. When Jenny learned Dustin and Caren had just adopted their first and only child, she sprang into action. Enlisting the help of the flight crew, Jenny secretly organized an impromptu baby shower. One crewmember casually asked Dustin and Caren a few personal questions, leaving them confused. But then a flight attendant came on the intercom and said, "Ladies and gentlemen, there's a very special guest on the flight today. She's only 8 days old and she's traveling home with her mom and dad."

After the passengers burst into applause, the crew passed out pens and napkins and encouraged them to jot down notes of advice, love, and encouragement. Some were read aloud. Many passengers stopped by to congratulate the new parents. After arriving home, Dustin contacted Southwest Airlines to offer his gratitude. "For an entire crew of strangers to come together like that, to partake like that, to show us that kind of love and kindness meant everything to us." If strangers, thrown together for a few hours, can organize a baby shower thousands of feet in the air, there may be no limit to the ways you and I can express God's manifold grace.

At this point, pause again, read the following questions, and then share your reflections in your journal or in conversation with a person you trust.

◆ ◆ ◆

Reflection Questions And Next Steps:

1. Take a few moments to reflect on your life. How have you experienced the Trinity serving you?
2. Read 1 Peter 4:9-10. How could you demonstrate gracious hospitality to someone else's odd-sounding ideas?
3. How might you be emotionally hospitable to someone outside your social circle?
4. Who could you serve, that they might become a hero?
5. Is there a person or organization it would be wise for you to serve financially?
6. Have you received a "gift" that you would really rather not have, but could use to serve others? If so, what is it – and whom could it help?
7. What or whom are you stewarding? How may God be resourcing you to be a faithful steward?

Honoring One Another

"Be devoted to one another in love. Honor one another above yourselves."

ROMANS 12:10

For a week, Washington, D.C. meteorologists had been keeping their eye on Hurricane Isabel as she moved in a northwesterly direction from the Southern Atlantic.[175] With winds of over 150 miles per hour, Isabel wreaked havoc as it sped toward the nation's capital.

On September 18, 2003, all federal government offices closed and most of Congress left town. Museums and monuments shut down as Washington's streets, usually jammed with tourists, emptied. Even the Metro subway closed.

As Hurricane Isabel bore down on Washington, D.C., heavy rains and winds over 50 miles per hour pelted the city. Trees toppled and 700,000 people were left without power.

Meanwhile, standing guard at the Tomb of the Unknowns in Arlington National Cemetery at the height of the storm, Sergeant 1st Class Fredrick Geary heard a sharp cracking sound. The tomb sentinel did not flinch as an old tree collapsed a couple of dozen yards away.

Geary could have retreated to shelter. As Isabel approached, commanders gave tomb guards the option to move under the shelter of the tomb's arches or even inside the trophy room during the storm.

That did not happen.

"Other than something earth-shattering, we had no intention of doing anything other than our duty," said Geary. As sergeant of the guard, he made the decision to keep the sentinels on the black mat that they walk 365 days a year, 24 hours a day.

The day after the storm hit, ground crews cleaned up 24 fallen trees at the cemetery, including two near the tomb and the sentinels.

Guarding the Tomb of the Unknowns is a duty the armed forces reserve for our finest soldiers. Since 1937, they have continuously guarded the tomb, dedicated to lost and missing American service members. Staff Sgt. Alfred Lanier, who was also on duty that night, explained, "Once you become a badge holder, it's like you'll do whatever you have to do to guard the unknowns. For one, it's my job. And for two, that's just how much respect I myself have for the unknowns. That's just something we cherish."

There is something inspiring about one person honoring another. The act elevates the person honored, the person honoring, and observers alike.

Paul begins Romans 12:9 reminding that love must be sincere, without hypocrisy. Then, in Romans 12:10, he uses two similar words. Behind "be devoted" is *philostorgos*, implying "tenderly loving".[176] This describes the affection for one's immediate family.[177] He also calls for *philadelphia*, warm, brotherly kindness and affection.[178]

Not everyone comes from a close-knit family, but some of us come to serve in organizations that understand the importance of honoring one another. As a pastor, I have led and attended my share of memorial services, but one stands out from the rest. When a local firefighter died and our church hosted the memorial service, I saw honor in a new light. Two large fire trucks drove into our parking lot, raised their long ladders, and lofted a giant U.S. flag. Many California Highway Patrol, local police, and deputy sheriffs attended in uniform. The service peoples' crisp, disciplined demeanor communicated their respect for this family and their service member.

Few people are more devoted to their craft than Alex Honnold.[179] In 2017, Honnold scaled Yosemite's El Capitan, a 3,000-foot granite rock considered the most challenging climbing wall in the world. He was the first person to make the climb "free solo" - without equipment or ropes, using only his body, hands, and feet. To immerse himself in climbing, he lives most of the year out of his van, saying:

> I want to climb in the best places in the world ... So I'm willing to give up having stability, having

> a shower, having whatever in order to climb the way that I want ... I am probably more intentional with the way I live my life than virtually anybody. I have made clear choices about what I find value in, what risks I am willing to take. I am doing exactly what I love to do. It's very easy for someone sitting on the couch at home to condemn it as crazy and stupid. But I can justify all my choices - can you say the same about your life?

Honnold's devotion to climbing can inspire us to examine our devotion to God - and to his people.

John Stott, rector of All Souls Langham Place in London, was one of the most devoted and influential Christian leaders of the twentieth century. Stott was known for his preaching, teaching, writing, evangelism, and development of Christian leaders around the world. In his book, *Impossible People*, Os Guinness describes a visit to Stott's bedside three weeks before his passing.[180]

> After an unforgettable hour and more of sharing many memories over many years, I asked him how he would like me to pray for him. Lying weakly on his back and barely able to speak, he answered in a hoarse whisper, "Pray that I will be faithful to Jesus until my last breath."

In our day, indifference and apathy are common. People describe themselves as "over it", "done" or "*so* done". Yet devotion to Christ and devotion to people enabled John Stott to make an unusually large impact.

Daniel James Brown's book *The Boys In The Boat* tells the heartwarming story of how nine underdog, working-class young men from Washington state upset elite rowers from the Ivy League and went on to the 1936 Berlin Olympics to defeat Adolf Hitler's rowers and win gold.[181] No one wins at rowing alone. Behind their success was a commitment to one another, a willingness to give up some of who they were to become something grander. Brown describes the teamwork involved in rowing this way:

> There is a thing that sometimes happens in rowing that is hard to achieve and hard to define ... It's called "swing." It only happens when all eight oarsmen are rowing in such perfect unison that no single action by any one is out of sync with those of all the others. ... Sixteen arms must begin to pull, sixteen knees must begin to fold and unfold, eight bodies must begin to slide forward and backward, eight backs must bend and straighten all at once. Each minute action - each subtle turning of wrists - must be mirrored exactly by each oarsman, from one end of the boat to the other. Only then will the boat continue to run, unchecked, fluidly and gracefully between pulls of the oars. Only then will it feel as if the boat is a part of each of them, moving as if on its own. Only then does pain entirely give way to exultation. Rowing then becomes a kind of perfect language. Poetry, that's what a good swing feels like.

The effectiveness of these rowers on the water derived from something in each heart. Their coach had led them to be devoted to one another.

To honor is to value. Honor can be described as an advantage believers assign to one another, rather than claiming it for themselves. This honor does not depend on status or intrinsic value but on being accepted by the Triune God.[182] Some have translated Romans 12:10 in part as "be eager to", "be quick to", "do not hesitate to", "be happy to", "be conspicuous to" or "outdo one another" in showing honor.[183]

Nishan Bakalian is a minister in Lebanon, who tells the following story.[184]

> In the town of Stepanavan, Armenia, I met a woman whom everyone called "Palasan's wife." She had her own name, of course, but townspeople called her by her husband's name to show her great honor. When the devastating 1988 earthquake struck Armenia, it was nearly noon, and Palasan was at work. He rushed to the elementary school where his son was a student.
>
> The facade was already crumbling, but he entered the building and began pushing children outside to safety. After Palasan had managed to help twenty-eight children out, an aftershock hit that completely collapsed the school building and killed him. So the people of Stepanavan honor his memory, and his young widow, by calling her "Palasan's wife".

The highest honor of any believer is to be called a disciple of Jesus Christ, who laid down his life for all people. As those Christ honored with his life and death, we have the resources to honor one another.

Too often, honor is delayed. Following the terrible attack on Pearl Harbor, Captain Joe Rochefort broke Japanese communication codes.[185] Stationed at an intelligence base in Oahu, he predicted the Japanese would attack Midway on June 3, 1942. They did. "He was a Japanese linguist, an intelligence analyst, and a cryptologist. [He had] the skills that enabled him to bring together the missing bits and pieces," said Rear Admiral Donald M. Showers. Because of Rochefort's expertise, the United States surprised the Japanese Navy with its first defeat in 350 years. Japan lost four carriers, one cruiser, over 2,500 men, over 240 aircraft, and their best pilots. Due to this crippling defeat, Japan eventually lost the war.

However, for his contribution, Rochefort was not recognized. Instead, intelligence men in Washington, D.C., falsified reports and claimed credit, even though they had predicted the attack would happen elsewhere and on a later date. Washington sealed the records for 40 years, and Rochefort was never properly rewarded. In fact, he was removed from intelligence and assigned to a floating dry dock in San Francisco.

Joseph J. Rochefort Jr., an Army captain and a graduate of West Point, said his father never complained about not being awarded the medal. "His attitude was, you can accomplish almost anything as long as nobody cares who gets the credit," he said.

People around us use rare combinations of skills to make significant contributions every day. Yet, they are not always recognized. Sometimes because of rivalry or envy, distraction or haste their accomplishments go overlooked. It is never too late to honor those deserving honor.

The 1962 film *To Kill a Mockingbird* stars Gregory Peck as Atticus Finch, a lawyer living in Macon, Georgia, during the 1940s.[186] Atticus is a widower, raising two children while operating a law practice. He defends a local black man, Tom Robinson, accused of raping a local young white woman. The lawyer mounts a noble defense that raises much doubt as to the defendant's guilt. However, most of the townspeople remain unconvinced. The father of the woman who was allegedly raped is outraged that Atticus would defend a black man.

After being tipped off that a mob is going to break into the jail and take the prisoner, Atticus sits outside the jail, guarding his client. Carloads of angry men arrive, some carrying rifles, and threaten Atticus. They demand he step aside. He stands firm.

After an emotional trial in which the accuser insists that the defendant is guilty and the accused tearfully proclaims his innocence, the all-white jury files back into the courtroom. Deliberations have concluded and a cloud of quiet anticipation settles over the segregated courtroom. The judge asks, "Gentlemen of the jury, have you reached a verdict?" The jurors reply, "Guilty." At first Atticus's eyes reveal shock and disbelief. But he then gathers himself and directs his concern toward his client, pleading with him to remain hopeful and patient, while vowing to appeal. Unfortunately, there would be no need for an appeal. Later that evening the sheriff notifies Atticus that while transferring Robinson, he tried to escape and was shot and killed.

As the courtroom clears and Atticus collects his papers, one by one the black townspeople, who are seated in the balcony along with Atticus' two children, stand out of respect. A black minister says to Atticus' daughter, "Miss Jean Louise. Miss Jean Louise. Stand up. Your father's passing."

As people who worship the God of all justice, in the face of earthly injustice, those who work for justice should be honored.

Take time now to reflect on the following questions. Share your thoughts in your journal or with someone you trust.

Reflection Questions And Next Steps:

1. Reflect on what the earthly life of Jesus tells you about the Trinity. What does this reveal

about how the members of the Trinity honor one another?

2. Read Romans 12:10. Who near you is making a significant contribution that you could honor?
3. How could you ask questions that illuminate others' honorable actions?
4. In your speech, how could you subtly honor others?
5. Are you aware of any unnoticed contributions you could now choose to recognize?
6. Could others perceive anything you say or do as dishonoring? How will you change that?
7. How does the timeliness, thoroughness, and tone of your emails, texts, and calls honor others?
8. If you did something honorable that other people overlooked, ridiculed, or even punished, how could Jesus' work on the cross speak to you?

4. ENGAGING OUR CULTURE

"I in them and you in me—so that they may be brought to complete unity. Then the world will know that you sent me and have loved them even as you have loved me."

JESUS, JOHN 17:23

We have come a long way.

After considering the divisiveness of our culture, we looked at how the nature of the Trinity resources us as people in relationships. Then we looked at six concrete New Testament commands to love, remain members of, demonstrate kindness to, encourage, serve and honor one another. Now we can ask: If a church reflects the Trinity and practices the "one anothers", what difference can it make in our culture?

Migliore reminds us that the Trinitarian nature

of God has implications for what God's people do in the world.[187] The members of the Triune God have not chosen to exist for themselves alone. Neither do the members of the church exist for themselves alone. The Triune God who lives in unending, mutual, self-giving love would include all creatures in that communion of love. The Triune God extends the Son of God and the Spirit of God into the world. The Spirit has breathed out the Word of God. This movement of God to the world means God is a missionary God. In God's mission to the world, the church finds the basis and model for its mission. Following the example of Christ, through the power of the Spirit and to the glory of the Father, the church is built up and sent into the world. The mission of the church is Christ-centered; it witnesses to the mission of the Son of God who came to inaugurate a new kingdom. The mission of the church is Spirit-led, carried out through the power of the Spirit of God. The same Spirit that came at Pentecost to increase communication and connection and to equip people for mission (Acts 2:1-41), today breaks down walls that separate people. Baptism into Christ by the power of the Spirit symbolizes one's incorporation into the community of faith where individuality is embraced as part of a rich unity.

In church history, and even today, there are contexts in which the mission of the church is understood primarily in political terms.[188] In these moments, the church has been called to speak to urgent political causes or social issues. And at times, to be faithful to Christ, the church must speak up in this way. However, in such moments, the church also runs the risk of allowing its mission to become politicized, and the field in which it effectively expresses its mission unacceptably narrowed. Rightly understood, the mission of the church rises not from the culture, nor from any issue in the culture, but from the nature of the Trinity. The mission of the church is expressed through the nature and behavior of people who correspond to the Trinity, in their personhood and relationships, even if in fallen and imperfect ways. With the light of the gospel of Christ, the church illumines all areas of contemporary life with implications for the pandemic, racial equality, the economy, and politics as well as for the family, education, media, the arts, and science. In such contexts, the church of the Son of God, inhabited by the Spirit of God, is characterized by love and service in which all share gifts given by God. Everyone in this reconciled community receives a new, transcendent identity in relation to the Trinity. Together, as a reconciling community, we express that identity as a sign of the coming reign of the Triune God.

The church has a high calling, and we face steep challenges, yet there are hopeful signs even in our country's electoral process. If democracy is, simply put, a system of government by the people and for the people, then the people governing should look something like the people governed. Increasingly, this is so: the racial and ethnic diversity of the U.S. Congress continues to approach the racial and ethnic diversity of the U.S. population. The Pew Research Center compared the 532 voting members of Congress, seated on January 26, 2021, with the U.S. population at that time.[189] Almost a quarter of voting members of the U.S. House of Representatives and Senate (23%) are racial or ethnic minorities, making the 117th Congress the most racially and ethnically diverse in history. This is the sixth Congress to break the diversity record set by the one before it. In January 2021, 124 lawmakers identified as Black, Hispanic, Asian/Pacific Islander, or Native American, according to data from the Congressional Research Service.

Although recent Congresses have shown increasing racial and ethnic diversity, they have still been disproportionately White compared with the overall U.S. population. Non-Hispanic White Americans account for 77% of voting members in the new Congress, considerably larger than their 60% share of the U.S. population. In the House of Representatives, however, representation of some racial and ethnic groups does now reflect their share of the total population. For example, 13% of House members are Black, about equal to the share of Black Americans. Native Americans now make up about 1% of the House and the U.S. population. Other racial and ethnic groups in the House are somewhat less represented, relative to their share of the population. The share of Hispanics in the U.S. population is 19%, about twice as high as it is in the House (9%). Asian Americans and Pacific Islanders account for 6% of the national population but just 3% of House members.

While this progress is encouraging, much work remains to be done in our divisive culture, work that reflects the very nature of God and that responds to the commands of Scripture. Let me point to four things each of us can do.

Listening

We often underestimate the power of listening, and for good reasons. Listening requires humility and security. While in some ways free, in other ways listening requires us to pay costs with our personhood, spending our energy and time, using our ears, eyes, and mind. Listening to views that are different from our own requires engaging another set of assumptions, starting points, logical sequences, and implications. Listening is an act of self-donation. Listening means making room for the existence and perspective of another. Listening gives significance to another but means being affected, to some degree, by another. Yet listening does not mean we agree with each thing that is said. Rather, it means hearing what is said, acknowledging it, and honoring it, simply because the person from whom it comes is made in the image of God.

As you consider the depth of communion the Father, Son, and Spirit experience and the other-serving community we are called to as Christians, how might you listen to people who are very different from you?

One initiative using the power of listening is Bridging the Gap. It is based in part on an idea in the book *Just Mercy* by civil rights lawyer Bryan Stevenson. The premise is that people on death row are more than the worst thing they have done.[190] Bridging the Gap applies that principle to our political culture, saying to millions of voters who voted one way, and to millions of voters who voted another way, that each voter is more than their vote. The program has been used on liberal and conservative college campuses to practice "deep listening", on the belief that engaging one another in humility and curiosity may help us solve the pressing issues of our time.[191]

Bridging the Gap founder Simon Greer writes,

> It might be hard to imagine engaging in deep listening across lines of difference. It might even seem counterintuitive. There is a legitimate fear that this "other" might not just disagree with you, or even fundamentally challenge your core values—they might actually be dangerous ... Even worse, our culture now appears to hold that listening to the other side, really listening, is considered a waste of time, at best, and at worst an act of infidelity or high treason.

In such a context, Bridging the Gap advances the notion that the heroes are the bridge-builders.

Greer writes:

> Listening deeply means silencing that noise, listening not just with your ears but with every sense you've got, every cell in your body. It means listening to all that is said and unsaid, to the body language, the tone, the eye movement. It's full-body listening. This type of listening builds trust, opens doors, and offers a path to deep discovery and a sacred connection that forms the basis for new understandings and otherwise unimaginable possibilities. Study after study shows in sector after sector—in medicine, marriage, real estate sales, and more—that true listening generates better results. And yet most of us go through our entire education without having learned how to do it.

Greer asks, if we decide to not engage deeply with those we may call the "other", then, what is our plan? "Unfriend everyone on social media who doesn't belong to your political party? Support your state in seceding from the union? Turn your home into a fortified bunker? Immigrate to Canada?" Or, we might add, move to an area with a more agreeable political climate? The problem with those approaches is they do not promise to solve any of our culture's significant problems. So before any of that - what if we doubled down on listening?

Consider the example of Daryl Davis.

Daryl Davis is a blues musician, with an interesting side gig. For over 30 years, Davis, who is Black, has intentionally listened to and befriended members of the Ku Klux Klan.[192] He says once a friendship develops, the Klansmen begin to question their hate. Since Davis started talking with them, he reports that 200 Klansmen have given up their robes. Davis collects the robes as a reminder of the possibilities that can open by simply sitting down with people and having dinner. Davis' parents are American, yet he spent part of his childhood overseas. From an early experience with racism in America, he has been motivated by the question: How can you hate me when you do not even know me?

Davis attends Klan rallies. He invites Klansmen to his home. He visits Klansmen in their homes. He calls some "friends" even as they call him inferior. *Accidental Courtesy*, a documentary describing Davis' work, recounts how Davis met the daughters of an incarcerated Klan member at the airport and drove them to a prison so they could visit their father. Eventually, their ideology of hate collapsed in the face of undeserved compassion.

Not everyone appreciates Davis' approach. In one of the documentary's most complex scenes, Davis is confronted by three Black community activists in Baltimore. They question whether his work has led to significant change or helped anyone who suffers under racism.

Still, Davis believes we will be better and stronger, healthier and happier as one nation than as a segregated one. Late in the documentary, Davis is asked what he feels as he watches a video of former racists who have left the Klan. Davis' reply is profound: "These are my fellow Americans."[193]

Davis listens to differences with surprising results. But it may be tempting to think, "That is him. I do not have his time or energy." For people like you and me, Rick Langer and Tim Muehlhoff lead The Winsome Conviction Project. Launched out of concern over the polarized communication climate affecting our culture and the church, they aim to encourage conversations in the church and the culture that deepen relationships and enrich lives, rather than divide. Their website includes resources that can help you and me be persuasive *and* civil, at the same time.[194]

James 1:19 reminds us, "Everyone should be quick to listen, slow to speak and slow to become angry." How might you become a deeper listener? How could you use sincere, open-ended questions to prompt people to share their inner thoughts with you? In this divisive age, how will you resource yourself to be an exceptional listener?

One thing you can do is to join me in praying this prayer.

Triune God,

Father, you have heard Jesus' prayers and you

have heard the groaning of the Spirit on my behalf. Help me now to use the faculties you have given me to listen well. Save me from my distractions. Save me from myself. Help me to set aside my own needs and wants and to listen deeply to where others are coming from, to what concerns them most, and to how they think things should go. Make me an engaging presence in the life of someone different from me. In Jesus' Name, Amen.

Learning

Listening is a start, but not a destination. Deep listening makes learning possible, but not inevitable. Sometimes, we don't want to learn. Learning can involve seeing things in a new light, changing our minds, and coming to a new understanding of our place in the world.

David Hubbard was one of my graduate school professors. He distinguished between accessing information and learning. He pointed out, even then, that we swim in a sea of information. But being surrounded by information is different from understanding, organizing, assimilating, and incorporating aspects of that information into one's mind, heart, and life. The latter is a demanding and often painful process in which we are changed.[195]

We are disciples of Christ. And the word disciple can mean student. We learn to live in the way of Christ. But that is not all we need to learn. We cannot be faithful to Christ while still embracing outdated cultural categories. The only place we can be disciples and make disciples for Christ is here and now. To live out our calling faithfully, we need to be students of our culture, to learn some things from it, if we are to engage it effectively. The second person of the Trinity was born into a human culture. Luke 2:52 reminds us the earthly "Jesus grew in wisdom." So can we.

One way we learn is to allow other Christians to express the "one anothers" to us. As others love, encourage, and serve us, we will learn about them - and from them. This personal porosity, being emotionally permeable, allowing others to influence us, does not weaken us but strengthens us.

Especially when it comes to race, many of us have an opportunity to learn from the Black Church. According to a Pew Research Center survey, some 75% of Black Americans say Black churches have helped promote racial equality.[196] Historically, Black churches have been places of dynamic worship - but have also brought vital support to their surrounding communities. They offer services such as job training programs and insurance cooperatives and many of their pastors advocate for racial equality. Black adults are more likely to say predominantly Black churches have helped Black people move toward equality in the U.S. than they are to say the same thing about the federal government or predominantly White churches. Black Americans attending Protestant churches where most attendees and leaders are Black were more likely to say they hear messages about social issues like race and politics than are Black Protestants who attend churches that are multiracial or largely White.[197]

In our hyper-mediated, increasingly divided age, as people have fewer relationships with people outside their ideological tribe, there is a tremendous need to learn directly from people who are different from us. Braver Angels is an organization that seeks to help Americans understand one another beyond stereotypes, reduce vitriol, and form community-based alliances. They focus on helping people understand others with whom they may disagree using principles that bring people together, rather than divide them, so they can work together for the common good.[198]

Paul learned from others, without giving up his convictions about Christ, in order to model and share his convictions about Christ. In 1 Corinthians 9:22 he wrote, "I have become all things to all people so that by all possible means I might save some." Paul learned. Paul adapted. So can we.

Would you pray this prayer?

Father God,

Thank you for creating the people of the rich culture in which I live. Even as I seek to be a disciple of Christ in things that matter most, help me to be a wise student of the passing culture in which I live, for the cause of Christ.

By your Spirit, enable me to engage those around me in winsome ways, that they would see and know your ways. Amen.

Loving

When it comes to love, each of us faces the challenge of overcoming our self. That is one reason reflecting on the perfect balance of identity and otherness, individuality and community in the Trinity can be so helpful. Presently, some of us are grieving lost influence in our culture. We should grieve. We have experienced loss. We should lament. But we should not give up hope because our hope is outside us. Our Hope has not dimmed in the least. The One in whom we hope is as loving as ever. Our culture is ever more in need of the hope we have in the Triune God. And it is precisely their self-donating love in which we "live and move and have our being" (Acts 17:28).

We often think of love as a feeling, rather than as an action. Love songs abound and touch us. But when we don't feel loving, we can get stuck. Long ago, Thomas Aquinas (1225-1274) wrote that "to love is to will the good of the other."[199] I find that perspective so helpful. Often because of my fallenness, and occasionally because of another's fallenness, I do not always feel loving toward someone else. But you and I always have the freedom to choose our actions. Even if I do not feel loving towards another person, I can choose actions that will benefit them. You and I can love people by what we will.

1 John 4:11 reminds us, “Beloved, if God so loved us, we also ought to love one another.” Reflecting on the nature of the Trinity and practicing the “one anothers” in Christian community, can resource us to love those around us. And there is good news, even in our divided age: one of the few things everyone wants more of is love.

◆ ◆ ◆

Could you pray this prayer?

Father, Son and Spirit,

Thank you for sharing your perfect love with me. As you loved me despite my sin, help me to love others today. When I struggle with aspects of others' lives that do not cause you to struggle, help me to take the humble path and to simply love. May the love you experience show up in my relationships today. Amen.

Leading

Leading in our divisive time seems more fraught than ever. Leading demands great energy, insight, and risk, yet our culture seems less forgiving, with ever more ways to fall afoul of others’ expectations.

But our God leads on. The Trinity *is* a missionary God. From the perfect unity of the Trinity, the Son was sent to live and teach, die, and be resurrected. From perfect community, the Spirit was sent to inhabit those who believe. As those called to "follow God's example, as dearly loved children and [to] walk in the way of love just as Christ loved us and gave himself up for us" (Ephesians 5:1-2), we are called to serve those in our culture at their point of need. Sincere service, putting others' needs above our own, leads to influence, which is the very essence of leadership.

And as God leads on, his people, made in his image, must lead on as well. Peter Northouse writes about leadership in a textbook used in over 1,600 academic institutions. While leadership has been described in a variety of ways, Northouse defines it as "a process whereby an individual influences a group of individuals to achieve a common goal."[200] The components of this definition illuminate what it means for us to lead in our culture.

Leadership is a process. It is not a trait. It is not a right. It is a dynamic that occurs between a leader and followers. It is not linear. It is not one-way. The leader affects followers and is affected by them. Leadership is not the exclusive domain of people with a title or a role; leadership is an interaction available to anyone. As the impacts of a post-Christian culture reveal themselves, it is important to remember that in our workplaces, schools, communities, and cultures we can bring leadership.

Leadership involves an individual. Because

each of us is distinct, our leadership will be informed by our unique traits, temperament, beliefs, skills, situation, cultural context, and behavior. We are not limited by or destined to repeat others' leadership results. Our leadership will look different from the leadership we read about in books.

Leadership is influence. Whatever else may vary in its many definitions, leadership involves how leaders communicate with and affect followers. Where there is no influence, there is no leadership. In a divisive time, we can value communication, protect relationships and continue to influence.

Leadership occurs in groups. Our culture abounds in groups, from small gatherings in homes to affinity groups, workgroups, recreational groups, online groups, and large, complex organizations. Each of them is the site of leadership. And to each group to which we belong, we can bring influence.

Leadership involves attention to common goals. Listening is so important because it allows us to identify the goals we hold in common with others. Leadership is never a function of just the leader, but a function of priorities the leader and followers share.

These leadership components can help us evaluate the impact of our leadership in the culture. If we are not connecting and communicating with others beyond the church, if we are not influencing people outside our sphere of belief, we are not bringing leadership to our culture. If we do not identify common goals, we do not lead.

As Christians, what we believe and practice because of our faith, deeply informs how we can lead. As we practice the "one anothers" with people who share our faith, we are trained in attractive ways to enter into a leadership process with those beyond our faith. As we understand the grounds of human personhood in the divine persons of the Trinity, we see the value and dignity of each leader - and of each potential leader. As we reflect on the sending of the Son of God and the Spirit of God into the world, we are empowered to strengthen connection and communication with people beyond our community of faith. When we reflect on the divine community within the Trinity, and the weak and faint ways the church can reflect that image, we are reminded the people of God can influence the many cultural groups to which we belong. And as the members of the Trinity are absolutely aligned and other-preferring, we can look for biblically-informed goals to pursue in tandem with members of our cultural community.

Northern Ireland is one place that has experienced its share of division. In the latter part of the twentieth century, it bred tension and bloodshed known as "The Troubles." The region contains a city so divided that part of the population calls it Derry while others call it Londonderry. In this city, Protestants (unionists) live on the east bank of the River Foyle, while Catholics (nationalists) live on the west bank. Though not far apart physically, many Protestants and Catholics live separate lives. They study at different schools, play different sports, go to different social gatherings and attend different churches. Few people cross these divides. So, innovators built a bridge. Now a 771-foot bridge for walkers, joggers, and cyclists spans the river, linking the two cities. It is named "Peace Bridge."[201] Building such a bridge was no small undertaking. It serves as a metaphor for the bridge-building we all can do, as ones called by the Triune God to lead out in love.

Hebrews 10:24 reminds us to "consider how we may spur one another on toward love and good deeds." Perhaps these acts would be well received by many.

Can you pray this prayer?

God in Heaven, God in me,

Just as you broke into this world in Christ, and continue to influence our world through your Spirit, deepen your work in me. Enable me to bring spiritual leadership to the circles of my life. Make me the type of listener that is humble and resilient, deep and patient. Allow me to learn chiefly from Christ, but also from those around me, who may be so different from me. From your limitless supply, give me love for other believers and for those who do not know you. Triune God, as you have influenced me allow me to influence others that your glory may grow and grow. Amen.

A FINAL WORD

We live in a fractious time.

Taking offense is more common even than giving offense. As we come into proximity and interact, we layer multiple "identities" related to our perspective on any number of issues including the pandemic, our race, our economic situation, and our political affiliation. It does not take much for division to happen yet again. However, we are not alone. At this very moment, the Triune God - Father, Son, and Spirit - an indescribable community of divine persons in relationships live together in other-preferring, self-donating love. Their identity is constituted by one another. Their community relies on one another. Scripture reminds us that every single person is made in their image - and that we who follow Christ are inhabited by their very Spirit. Time and again, Scripture commands us, as followers of Jesus, to practice the "one anothers", which include loving one another, remaining members of one another, being kind to one another, encouraging one another, serving one another, and honoring one another. You and I, as followers of Christ, are linked to one another and other Christians by an indissoluble spiritual bond. The way we treat one another, and the earthly unity that results, will enable our world to know that the Father sent the Son into this world and that the Father loves this world, even as he loves Jesus his Son. Indwelt by the Spirit and informed by Scripture, we can continue expressing these "one anothers" to people of faith in Christ, and engaging people beyond our circle of faith with deep and patient listening, with humble and sincere learning, with sacrificial and generous loving, and with gentle yet courageous leading.

Our culture desperately needs this kind of influence. We were *made* for this. This is *our* moment. Because the One who is in us is greater than the one who is in the world (1 John 4:4), we *can* do this. I commend you to it.

May others be blessed. May your joy overflow. And may God be glorified.

APPENDIX: SELECT "ONE ANOTHER" PASSAGES FROM THE NEW TESTAMENT

John 13:14 If I then, your Lord and Teacher, have washed your feet, you also ought to wash one another's feet.

John 13:34 A new commandment I give to you, that you love one another: just as I have loved you, you also are to love one another.

John 13:35 By this all people will know that you are my disciples, if you have love for one another.

John 15:12 This is my commandment, that you love one another as I have loved you.

John 15:17 These things I command you, so that you will love one another.

Romans 12:5 We, though many, are one body in Christ, and individually members one of another.

Romans 12:10 Love one another with brotherly affection. Outdo one another in showing honor.

Romans 12:16 Live in harmony with one another. Do not be haughty, but associate with the lowly. Never be wise in your own sight.

Romans 13:8 Owe no one anything, except to love each other, for the one who loves another has fulfilled the law.

Romans 14:13 Therefore let us not pass judgment on one another any longer, but rather decide never to put a stumbling block or hindrance in the way of a brother.

Romans 15:5 May the God of endurance and encouragement grant you to live in such harmony with one another, in accord with Christ Jesus,

Romans 15:7 Therefore welcome one another as Christ has welcomed you, for the glory of God.

Romans 15:14 I myself am satisfied about you, my brothers, that you yourselves are full of goodness, filled with all knowledge and able to instruct one another.

Romans 16:16 Greet one another with a holy kiss.

1 Corinthians 11:33 So then, my brothers, when you come together to eat, wait for one another—

2 Corinthians 13:12 Greet one another with a holy kiss.

Galatians 5:15 But if you bite and devour one another, watch out that you are not consumed by one another.

Galatians 5:26 Let us not become conceited, provoking one another, envying one another.

Galatians 6:2 Bear one another's burdens, and so fulfill the law of Christ.

Ephesians 4:2 with all humility and gentleness, with patience, bearing with one another in love,

Ephesians 4:25 Therefore, having put away falsehood, let each one of you speak the truth with his neighbor, for we are members one of another.

Ephesians 4:32 Be kind to one another, tenderhearted, forgiving one another, as God in Christ forgave you.

Ephesians 5:19 addressing one another in psalms and hymns and spiritual songs, singing and making melody to the Lord with your heart,

Ephesians 5:21 submitting to one another out of reverence for Christ.

Colossians 3:9 Do not lie to one another, seeing that you have put off the old self with its practices

Colossians 3:13 bearing with one another and, if one has a complaint against another, forgiving each other; as the Lord has forgiven you, so you also must forgive.

Colossians 3:16 Let the word of Christ dwell in you richly, teaching and admonishing one another in all wisdom, singing psalms and hymns and spiritual songs, with thankfulness in your hearts to God.

1 Thessalonians 3:12 and may the Lord make you increase and abound in love for one another and for all, as we do for you,

1 Thessalonians 4:9 Now concerning brotherly love you have no need for anyone to write to you, for you yourselves have been taught by God to love one another,

1 Thessalonians 4:18 Therefore encourage one another with these words.

1 Thessalonians 5:11 Therefore encourage one another and build one another up, just as you are doing.

1 Thessalonians 5:15 See that no one repays anyone evil for evil, but always seek to do good to one another and to everyone.

Hebrews 3:13 But exhort one another every day, as long as it is called "today," that none of you may be hardened by the deceitfulness of sin.

Hebrews 10:24 And let us consider how to stir up one another to love and good works

Hebrews 10:25 not neglecting to meet together, as is the habit of some, but encouraging one another, and all the more as you see the Day drawing near.

James 4:11 Do not speak evil against one another, brothers. The one who speaks against a brother or judges his brother, speaks evil against the law and judges the law. But if you judge the law, you are not a doer of the law but a judge.

James 5:9 Do not grumble against one another, brothers, so that you may not be judged; behold, the Judge is standing at the door.

James 5:16 Therefore, confess your sins to

one another and pray for one another, that you may be healed. The prayer of a righteous person has great power as it is working.

1 Peter 1:22 Having purified your souls by your obedience to the truth for a sincere brotherly love, love one another earnestly from a pure heart,

1 Peter 4:8 Above all, keep loving one another earnestly, since love covers a multitude of sins.

1 Peter 4:9 Show hospitality to one another without grumbling.

1 Peter 4:10 As each has received a gift, use it to serve one another, as good stewards of God's varied grace:

1 Peter 5:5 Clothe yourselves, all of you, with humility toward one another, for "God opposes the proud but gives grace to the humble."

1 Peter 5:14 Greet one another with the kiss of love. Peace to all of you who are in Christ.

1 John 1:7 But if we walk in the light, as he is in the light, we have fellowship with one another, and the blood of Jesus his Son cleanses us from all sin.

1 John 3:11 For this is the message that you have heard from the beginning, that we should love one another.

1 John 3:23 And this is his commandment, that we believe in the name of his Son Jesus Christ and love one another, just as he has commanded us.

1 John 4:7 Beloved, let us love one another, for love is from God, and whoever loves has been born of God and knows God.

1 John 4:11 Beloved, if God so loved us, we also ought to love one another.

1 John 4:12 No one has ever seen God; if we love one another, God abides in us and his love is perfected in us.

2 John 5 And now I ask you, dear lady—not as though I were writing you a new commandment, but the one we have had from the beginning—that we love one another.

ACKNOWLEDGMENTS

At William Jessup University, early on my colleagues Matt Godshall and Mark Moore provided helpful dialogue and recommendations. Near the end of the project, my colleague Jorge Luna provided encouraging and helpful feedback. Our librarians, Belinda Silva and Michael Kares, delivered quick and competent research support. Tammie Lovvorn, in our Writing Center, assisted with formatting. Jim Crain and Jules Binder provided valuable proofreading. Our Dean of the School of Theology and Leadership David Timms, delivered valuable coaching, questions, and encouragement throughout the project. Despite their help, any errors here are my responsibility alone.

When I was 17 years old, Carlo Walth began mentoring me. I am so glad for his influence and friendship since then, his feedback on this project, and the current iteration of our relationship as Jessup colleagues. It was a joy to write with our sons Noah, Jonah and Joshua at home working remotely, doing research and writing, and working in our community, respectively. You are wonderful co-workers. Finally, my wife Alyse patiently listened to, read, and discussed many of these points as only she can, for which I am deeply grateful.

NOTES

1. Division

[1] Just, S., (2020, February 6). *3 historians on American political divisiveness -- and how to heal it.* PBS NewsHour. https://www.youtube.com/watch?v=C3olsPSAElk&t=15s. In the NewsHour discussion, these points are made by historians Michael Beschloss and Ellen Fitzpatrick, respectively. Throughout I use the terms "divide", "division", "divisive", and "divisiveness" to describe the repeated fracturing of social bonds and the resultant fragmentation occurring in North American culture. Sometimes the result is political polarization along two competing alternatives. At other times, the result is a shattering of unity and a scattering without the institution of new order.

[2] Eberstadt, M. (2016, June 29). *Regular Christians are no longer welcome in American culture.* Time. https://time.com/4385755/faith-in-america/

[3] (2015, November 3). *U.S. public becoming less religious.* Pew Research Center.

https://www.pewforum.org/2015/11/03/u-s-public-becoming-less-religious/. The Pew Research Center describes itself as a nonpartisan fact tank that informs the public about the issues, attitudes and trends shaping the world. They conduct public opinion polling, demographic research, content analysis and other data-driven social science research. They do not take policy positions. See https://www.pewresearch.org/about/.

[4] Deane, C., Parker, K. & Gramlich, J., (2021, March 5). *A Year of U.S. public opinion on the Coronavirus pandemic.* Pew Research Center. https://www.pewresearch.org/2021/03/05/a-year-of-u-s-public-opinion-on-the-coronavirus-pandemic/

[5] Van Kessel, P. & Quinn, D. (2020, October 29). *Both republicans and democrats cite masks as a negative effect of COVID-19, but for very different reasons.* Pew Research Center. https://www.pewresearch.org/fact-tank/2020/10/29/both-republicans-and-democrats-cite-masks-as-a-negative-effect-of-covid-19-but-for-very-different-reasons/

[6] French, D., (2021, June 21). Can we escape the vaccine culture war? *Time.* p. 28-29. https://time.com/6071909/covid-19-vaccine-culture-war/. See also French, D. (2020) *Divided we fall: America's succession threat and how to restore our nation* by St. Martin's Press in which David French insightfully describes our nation's troubling divisiveness, envisions chilling scenarios that could lead to secession, and calls for enactment of James Madison's vision of pluralistic federalism.

[7] Dimock, M. & Wike, R., (2020, November 13). *America is exceptional in the nature of its political divide.* Pew Research Center. https://www.pewresearch.org/fact-tank/2020/11/13/america-is-exceptional-in-the-nature-of-its-political-divide/

[8] Deane, C., Parker, K. & Gramlich, J., (2021, March 5).

[9] Horowitz, J. M., Parker, K., Brown, A., & Cox, K., (2020, October 6). *Amid national reckoning, Americans divided on whether increased focus on race will lead to major policy change.* Pew Research Center. https://www.pewresearch.org/social-trends/2020/10/06/amid-national-reckoning-americans-divided-on-whether-increased-focus-on-race-will-lead-to-major-policy-change/#fnref-29180-1.

[10] O'Keefe, V. M. & Walls M. L. (2021, April 2). *Indigenous communities demonstrate innovation and strength despite unequal losses during COVID-19.* The Brooking Institution. https://www.brookings.edu/blog/how-we-rise/2021/04/02/indigenous-communities-demonstrate-innovation-and-strength-despite-unequal-losses-during-covid-19/. The Brookings Institution describes itself as a nonprofit public policy organization based in Washington, DC. Their mission is to conduct in-depth research that leads to new ideas for solving problems facing society at the local, national and global level. https://www.brookings.edu/about-us/.

[11] Horowitz, J. M., Brown, A., & Minkin, R. (2021, March 5). *A year into the pandemic, long-*

term financial impact weighs heavily on many Americans. Pew Research Center. https://www.pewresearch.org/social-trends/2021/03/05/a-year-into-the-pandemic-long-term-financial-impact-weighs-heavily-on-many-americans/

[12] Horowitz, J. M., Brown, A., & Minkin, R. (2021, March 5).

[13] Horowitz, J. M., Brown, A., & Minkin, R. (2021, March 5).

[14] Dunn, A., Kiley, J., Scheller, A., Baronavski, C., & Doherty, C., (2020, December 17). Voters say those on the other side 'don't get' them. Here's what they want them to know. Pew Research Center. https://www.pewresearch.org/politics/2020/12/17/voters-say-those-on-the-other-side-dont-get-them-heres-what-they-want-them-to-know/. While Republicans and Democrats continue to diverge on factors they see as important for being "truly American", such as being Christian or being born in the U.S., in both parties, the percentage of people who see these and other factors as important decreased from 2016 to November 2020. Connaughton, A. (2021, May 25). *In both parties, fewer now say being Christian or being born in U.S. is important to being 'truly American'.* Pew Research Center. https://pewrsr.ch/3vnbroP

[15] Dimock, M. & Wike, R., (2020, November 13).

[16] Dunn, A., Kiley, J., Scheller, A., Baronavski, C., & Doherty, C., (2020, December 17). *Voters say those on the other side 'don't get' them. Here's what they want them to know.* Pew Research Center. https://www.pewresearch.org/politics/2020/12/17/voters-say-those-on-the-other-side-dont-get-them-heres-what-they-want-them-to-know/.

[17] The U.S. is not the only country grappling with political divides. Brexit has polarized British politics and populist parties have disrupted party systems across Europe. Many advanced economies, including the United States, navigate tensions over the distribution of opportunity in a global economy and how culture adapts to the increased diversity brought about by greater interconnectedness. See Dimock, M. & Wike, R., (2020, November 13). *America is exceptional in the nature of its political divide.* Pew Research Center. https://www.pewresearch.org/fact-tank/2020/11/13/america-is-excep-

tional-in-the-nature-of-its-political-divide/

[18] Muir, W. M. and Cheng, H. W. (2014). Genetic Influences on the Behavior of Chickens Associated with Welfare and Productivity. In T. Grandin, & M. J. Deesing (Eds.) *Genetics and the Behavior of Domestic Animals, 2nd edition.* Academic Press. P. 317-359. https://doi.org/10.1016/C2011-0-07148-X

[19] Dimock, M. & Wike, R., (2020, November 13).

[20] Mitchell, A., Jurkowitz, M., Oliphant, J. B., & Shearer, E., (2021, February 22) *Misinformation and competing views of reality abounded throughout 2020.* Pew Research Center. https://www.journalism.org/2021/02/22/misinformation-and-competing-views-of-reality-abounded-throughout-2020/

[21] Dimock, M. & Wike, R., (2020, November 13).

[22] Volf, M. (2019). *Exclusion and embrace, revised and updated: A theological exploration of identity, otherness, and reconciliation.* Abingdon Press. p. xvii.

[23] Volf, M. (2019). P. xvii.

2. What Is God Like?

[24] Tozer, A. W. (2021) *Knowledge of the holy.* Sanage Publishing House. https://www.goodreads.com/quotes/376518-what-comes-into-our-minds-when-we-think-about-god. Tozer also writes here, “We tend by a secret law of the soul to move toward our mental image of God. This is true not only of the individual Christian, but of the company of Christians that composes the Church. Always the most revealing thing about the Church is her idea of God.”

[25] Throughout, this project uses the NIV 2011 version of the Bible.

[26] Bratcher, R. G., & Hatton, H. A. (2000). *A handbook on Deuteronomy.* United Bible Societies. p. 138.

[27] Grudem, W. A. (2004). *Systematic theology: an introduction to biblical doctrine.* Inter-Varsity Press; Zondervan Pub. House. pp. 227–229

[28] Grudem, W. A. (2004). pp. 227

[29] "My mouth speaks what is true, for my lips detest wickedness. All the words of my mouth are just; none of them is crooked or perverse." Proverbs 8:7-8; "Counsel and sound judgment are mine; I have insight, I have power." Proverbs 8:14; "I walk in the way of righteousness" Proverbs 8:20; "From eternity I was established,

From the beginning, from the earliest times of the earth." Proverbs 8:23-24.

[30] Letham, R., (2008) Trinity, Triune God, In W. A. Dyrness & V. Kärkkäinen, (Eds.) *Global Dictionary of Theology.* IVP Academic. p. 902.

[31] On this theme of more than one divine person being called Lord, see also Hosea 1:7, Isaiah 48:16 and Isaiah 61:1.

[32] Grudem, W. A. (2004). pp. 230–231

[33] For those interested in the Hebrew and Greek terms mentioned and how they are used elsewhere in the Bible, I include their transliteration.

[34] For a brief introduction to the Nicene Creed of 325 AD and the Nicene-Constantinopolitan Creed of 381 AD, see Migliore, D. L. (2014). *Faith seeking understanding: An introduction to christian theology, Third Ed..* Eerdmans. pp. 459-460.

[35] Historically, there are three main errors around Trinitarian thinking, according to Grudem. Modalism, sometimes referred to as modalistic monarchianism or Sabellianism, is the heretical teaching that God is not actually three distinct persons, but only one person who appears to people in different modes at different times. This is an easy error to fall into, for example claiming that in the Old Testament God appeared as "the Father", in the Gospels God appeared as "the Son" and after Pentecost this same person revealed himself as "the Spirit" active in the church. Modalism is attractive because it emphasizes there is one God, but it discounts Scriptures describing the personal relationships within the Trinity. Arianism is the heretical belief that denies the deity of the Son and Spirit. It led to the Nicene Creed of 325 AD. Arians depend on texts describing Christ as God's only begotten son yet give less credence to texts describing Christ as God. Tritheism, while less common, is the heretical view that there

are three divine persons, and each is fully God, so there are three Gods, not One. Grudem, W. A. (2004). pp. 242-248. For more on these three errors, see also, Migliore, D. L. (2014). pp. 458, 443 and 470, respectively.

[36] Migliore, D. L. (2014). pp. 76-77. See also Niebuhr, H. R., (1983). Theological Unitarianisms. *Theology Today* 40. pp. 150-57.

[37] Migliore, D. L. (2014). p. 76.

[38] Migliore, D. L. (2014). p. 76.

[39] Migliore, D. L. (2014). pp. 76-77.

[40] Letham, R. (2008) p. 906.

[41] Grenz, S. J. (1994). *Theology for the community of God.* Eerdmans. p. 80.

[42] Reeves, Michael (2012). *Delighting in the Trinity: An introduction to the Christian faith.* InterVarsity Press. p. 9.

[43] Reeves, Michael (2012). p. 10.

[44] Grudem, W. A. (2004). p. 226.

[45] For more on the Spirit as a person, rather than a mere "power" or "force", see Grudem, W. A. (2004). pp. 232-233.

[46] Grudem, W. A. (2004). p. 226.

[47] Migliore, D. L. (2014). p. 469.

[48] Volf, M. (1998). *After our likeness: The church as the image of the Trinity.* Eerdmans. pp. 192-193.

[49] Letham, R., (2008). p. 906. Modalism and Unitarianism of the Creator, described above, are two possible heretical views behind such universalization.

[50] See also for example John 7:16 where Jesus is recorded saying, "My teaching is not mine but his who sent me."

[51] Migliore, D. L. (2014). p. 462. Occasionally, to express the idea of mutual interpenetration (*perichoresis*) one will also see the Latin term *circumincessio*.

[52] Migliore, D. L. (2014). p. 443.

[53] Volf, M. (2019). p. 86.

[54] Ince, I. L. (2020). *The beautiful community: Unity, diversity, and the church at its best.* InterVarsity Press. p. 38.

[55] Migliore, D L. (2014). p. 82.

[56] Carr, A. E., (1988) *Transforming grace: Christian tradition and women's experience.* Harper and Row. pp. 156–57.

[57] Ashame, B., (2021, June 20th). Yanks tie record with 3rd triple play of '21. MLB.com. https://www.mlb.com/news/yankees-turn-third-triple-play-of-season-for-series-win.

[58] Volf, M. (2019). pp. 343-368.

[59] A recent contribution to this conversation, exploring hierarchical perspectives, is Barrett, M. (2021). *Simply Trinity: The unmanipulated Father, Son and Spirit.* Baker Books.

[60] Kärkkäinen, V.-M., (2008) Trinity, Triune God, In W. A. Dyrness & V. Kärkkäinen, V.-M. (Eds.) *Global dictionary of theology* (pp. 901-913). IVP Academic. pp. 908, 912.

[61] Then God said, "Let us make mankind in our image, in our likeness, so that they may rule over the fish in the sea and the birds in the sky, over the livestock and all the wild animals, and over all the creatures that move along the ground." So God created mankind in his own image, in the image of God he created them; male and female he created them." (Genesis 1:26-27)

[62] Volf, M. (2019). p. 343-368.

[63] The Trinity-human correspondence is based on what scholars refer to as the economic Trinity, rather than on the immanent Trinity. While there is one Trinity, the term "economic Trinity" refers to the engagement of the Father, Son and Spirit with earthly, salvation history. The term "immanent Trinity" refers to the eternal, essential and ontological aspects of the Trinity. Migliore writes, "If talk of the triune God is not to be wild speculation, it will always find its basis and its limit in the biblical narrative of the love of God that comes to the world through Jesus Christ in the power of the Holy Spirit who has poured God's love into our hearts" (Romans 5:5). Migliore, D L. (2014). p. 71.

[64] Volf, M. (1998). pp. 199-200.

[65] Volf, M. (1998). p. 239.

[66] Volf, M. (1998). pp. 206-207.

[67] Volf, M. (1998). p. 219.

[68] Volf, M. (2019). pp. 343-368.

[69] Augustine may have spent more effort wrestling with the mystery of the Trinity than anyone. He is credited with saying, "If you comprehend something, it is not God." See Migliore, D. L. (2014). p. 77.

[70] Volf, M. (2019). pp. 343-368.

[71] Migliore, D L. (2014). 272-273.

[72] Volf, M. (2019). pp. 343-368.

[73] Migliore, D L. (2014). pp. 73-74

[74] Kärkkäinen, V.-M., (2008) Trinity, Triune God, In W. A. Dyrness & V. Kärkkäinen, V.-M. (Eds.) *Global dictionary of theology* (pp. 901-913). IVP Academic. pp. 907-908.

[75] Volf, M. (2019). p. 343-368.

[76] Gunton, C. (1993). *The one, the three and the many.* Cambridge University Press.

[77] Volf, M. (2019). pp. 343-368.

[78] Ince, I. L. (2020). pp. 39.

[79] Volf, M. (1998). pp. 222-233.

[80] Grenz, S. J. (1994). p. 179.

[81] Grenz, S. J. (1994). p. 187.

[82] Grenz, S. J. (1994). p. 489.

[83] Migliore, D. L. (2014). p. 80.

[84] Migliore, D. L. (2014. p. 83.

[85] Migliore, D. L. (2014. pp. 272-273.

[86] https://www.goodreads.com/quotes/812389-the-reason-the-mass-of-men-fear-god-and-at

[87] While discussions continue, there is an emerging perspective that the biblical narrative reveals the Trinity, that the Trinity represents true personhood and true communion, that the Trinity is the structure of theology, and that the Trinity speaks to many contexts and needs at personal and communal levels. See Kärkkäinen, V.-M., (2008). p. 912.

[88] Some of these questions are adapted from Grudem, W. A. (2004). p. 258.

3. What Can The Church Be Like?

[89] Ephesians 1:22 and 5:23 describe Jesus Christ as the head of the church.

[90] Vine, W. E., Unger, M. F., & White, W., Jr. (1996). *Vine's complete expository dictionary of old and new testament words (Vol. 2).* T. Nelson. p. 40.

[91] See Beasley-Murray, G. R. (1999). *John (Vol. 36).* (Metzger, B. M., Hubbard, D. A., & Barker, G. W., general editors). Word, Incorporated. p. 302–303. In this section, I lean heavily on the work of Beasley-Murray.

[92] Newman, B. M., & Nida, E. A. (1993). *A handbook on the Gospel of John.* United Bible Societies. p. 544.

[93] Beasley-Murray, G. R. (1999). pp. 302–303.

[94] Beasley-Murray, G. R. (1999). pp. 302–303.

[95] Beasley-Murray, G. R. (1999). pp. 302–303.

[96] Beasley-Murray, G. R. (1999). pp. 302–303.

[97] Adapted from https://www.preachingtoday.com/illustrations/2018/february/holocaust-prisoners-survived-by-mutual-self-sacrifice.html. See also Moorehead, C., (2011) *A train in winter.* HarperCollins Publishers.

[98] Beasley-Murray, G. R. (1999). pp. 263-264.

[99] Getz, Gene (1981) *Building up one another.* Victor Books. p. 4.

[100] Louw, J. P., & Nida, E. A. (1996). *Greek-English lexicon of the new testament: based on semantic domains. Vol. 1.* United Bible Societies. p. 655.

[101] Raymer, R. M. (1985). 1 Peter. In J. F. Walvoord & R. B. Zuck (Eds.), *The Bible knowledge commentary: An exposition of the scriptures (Vol. 2).* Victor Books. p. 853.

[102] Michaels, J. R. (1988). *1 Peter (Vol. 49)*. (Metzger, B. M., Hubbard, D. A., & Barker, G. W., general editors). Word, Incorporated. p. 246.

[103] Arichea, D. C., & Nida, E. A. (1980). *A handbook on the first letter from Peter.* United Bible Societies. pp. 139–140. See also Proverbs 10:12, "Hatred stirs up conflict, but love covers over all wrongs."

[104] Stone, L., (2020, March 13). *Christianity has been handling epidemics for 200 years.* Foreign Policy. https://foreignpolicy.com/2020/03/13/christianity-epidemics-2000-years-should-i-still-go-to-church-coronavirus/.

[105] Stone, L., (2020, March 13).

[106] Brooks. A. C. (2020, October 22). *Are we trading our happiness for modern comforts?* The Atlantic. https://www.theatlantic.com/family/archive/2020/10/why-life-has-gotten-more-comfortable-less-happy/616807/. You may be interested in Brooks, A. C. (2016, February). *A conservative's plea: Let's work together.* [Video]. TED Conferences. https://www.youtube.com/watch?v=87AEeLpodnE (14:05)

[107] Vaillant, G., (2012). *Triumphs of experience: The men of the Harvard grant study*. Belknap Press.

[108] Brooks. A. C. (2020, October 22). *Are we trading our happiness for modern comforts?* The Atlantic. https://www.theatlantic.com/family/archive/2020/10/why-life-has-gotten-more-comfortable-less-happy/616807/.

[109] For more on the Harvard Study of Adult Development see https://www.adultdevelopmentstudy.org/. See also Waldinger, R. (2015, November). *What makes a good life? Lessons from the longest study on happiness.* [Video] TED Conferences. https://www.ted.com/talks/robert_waldinger_what_makes_a_good_life_lessons_from_the_longest_study_on_happiness?language=en#t-6291 (12:28)

[110] Forde, P., (2016, June 21). *Meet Maya DiRado, the 'late-blooming' phenom who could star for U.S. in Rio.* Yahoo!Sports. https://sports.yahoo.com/news/why-maya-dirado-23-will-retire-from-swimming-after-olympics-191215752.html. And Lee, M., (2016, August 5). *Meet the Rio Olympians Who Put God Before Gold.* Christianity Today. https://www.christianitytoday.com/

ct/2016/august-web-only/meet-rio-olympians-who-put-god-before-gold.html

[111] Bryce, R. (2018). *The fingerprint of god.* Brown Christian Press. pp. 55-56.

[112] Dunn, J. D. G. (1988). *Romans 9–16 (Vol. 38B).* (Metzger, B. M., Hubbard, D. A., & Barker, G. W., general editors). Word, Incorporated. pp. 724–725.

[113] In the New Testament, Paul used the word "body" (*soma* in Greek) more than 30 times to illustrate the functioning church. Getz, G. (1981). pp. 7, 9.

[114] Dunn, J. D. G. (1988). pp. 733.

[115] Lipka, M. & Gecewicz, C. (2017, September 6). *More Americans now say they're spiritual but not religious.* Pew Research Center. https://www.pewresearch.org/fact-tank/2017/09/06/more-americans-now-say-theyre-spiritual-but-not-religious/

[116] King, H., (2011, October 23) "The Better Church," *Shirt of Flame* blog. https://www.heather-king.com/arts-and-culture/

[117] Khan, A. (2011, April 29) Mystery of floating fire ants solved. *Los Angeles Times.* https://www.latimes.com/archives/la-xpm-2011-apr-29-la-sci-ants-raft-20110430-story.html

[118] Peterson, E., (2011). *The pastor.* HarperOne. pp. 95.

[119] https://www.preachingtoday.com/illustrations/2012/february/3021312.html

[120] May, C. (2014, October 14). The surprising problem of too much talent. *Scientific American.* https://www.scientificamerican.com/article/the-surprising-problem-of-too-much-talent/

[121] Vine, W. E., Unger, M. F., & White, W., Jr. (1996).. 63.

[122] Peterson, E. (1985). *Earth and altar: The community of prayer in a self-bound society.* InterVarsity Press.

[123] (1986). *Leadership Journal, 7*(3). https://www.christianitytoday.com/pastors/1986/summer/

[124] Parker, M. (2018, November 20). *Good samaritan returns lost wallet and adds money to it: 'I rounded your cash up to an even $100 so you could celebrate'.* Yahoo!Life. https://www.

yahoo.com/entertainment/good-samaritan-returns-lost-wallet-adds-money-rounded-cash-even-100-celebrate-223932122.html

[125] (2021, June 22) Whiting-Turner Contracting Company Newsletter. https://marketing-whiting-turner.foleon.com/stories/willard-hackerman/stories/. For more on the power of kindness see Mouw, R. (2010). *Uncommon decency: Christian civility in an uncivil world.* InterVarsity Press.

[126] Vine, W. E., Unger, M. F., & White, W., Jr. (1996). *Vine's complete expository dictionary of old and new testament words (Vol. 2).* T. Nelson. p. 472.

[127] Bratcher, R. G., & Nida, E. A. (1993). *A handbook on Paul's letter to the Ephesians.* United Bible Societies. p. 121.

[128] Muggeridge, Kitty (1985) *Gazing on truth: Meditations on reality.* Eerdmans.

[129] (1990). *Leadership Journal, 11*(3). https://www.christianitytoday.com/pastors/1990/summer/

[130] Berdyaev, Nicolai (1959) *The Origin of Russian communism.* University of Michigan Press.

[131] Louw, J. P., & Nida, E. A. (1996). *Greek-English lexicon of the New Testament: based on semantic domains electronic ed. of the 2nd edition. (Vol. 1).* United Bible Societies. p. 502.

[132] Hartman, S., (2011, June 8). *Love thy neighbor: Son's killer moves next door.* CBS News. https://www.cbsnews.com/news/love-thy-neighbor-sons-killer-moves-next-door/. For more on Mary Johnson and Oshea Israel see https://www.theforgivenessproject.com/stories/mary-johnson-oshea-israel/.

[133] Lincoln, A. T. (1990). *Ephesians (Vol. 42).* (Metzger, B. M., Hubbard, D. A., & Barker, G. W., general editors). Word, Incorporated. pp. 309–310.

[134] (2017, October 30). Maui judge orders man to write 144 nice things about ex-girlfriend. *Associated Press.* https://apnews.com/article/26a1d8f4a4694191880467cdaf8d0255

[135] Edmunds, D. R., (2020, August 16), 25% of young Americans are considering suicide amid coronavirus. *The Jerusalem Post.* https://www.jpost.com/health-science/quarter-of-young-americans-are-feeling-suicidal-driven-by-cor-

onavirus-638804. Czeisler M. É. , Lane R. I., Petrosky, E., et al. (2020, August 14). *Mental Health, Substance Use, and Suicidal Ideation During the COVID-19 Pandemic.* Centers for Disease Control and Prevention Morbidity Mortality Weekly Report. https://www.cdc.gov/mmwr/volumes/69/wr/mm6932a1.htm?s_cid=mm6932a1_w.%20Accessed%20March%2016,%202021.#

[136] Bruce, F. F. (1982). *1 and 2 Thessalonians (Vol. 45).* (Metzger, B. M., Hubbard, D. A., & Barker, G. W., general editors). Word, Incorporated. p. 115.

[137] Vine, W. E., Unger, M. F., & White, W., Jr. (1996). *Vine's complete expository dictionary of old and new testament words (Vol. 2).* T. Nelson. p. 62.

[138] Jeffreys, M. A. (1995). The Apostle Paul and His Times: A Gallery of Paul's Inner Circle. *Christianity Today/Christian History.* https://www.christianitytoday.com/history/issues/issue-47/apostle-paul-and-his-times-gallery-of-pauls-inner-circle.html

[139] Deabler, A., (2019, August 9). *Southwest passenger comforts frightened 96-year-old woman: He 'was her flight angel'.* Fox News. https://www.foxnews.com/travel/southwest-passenger-comforts-old-woman-flight-angel

[140] Youngmisuk, O., (2020, August 25). *Clippers' Paul George says he dealt with anxiety, depression inside NBA bubble.* ESPN. https://www.espn.com/nba/story/_/id/29743235/clippers-paul-george-says-dealt-anxiety-depression-bubble

[141] Vine, W. E., Unger, M. F., & White, W., Jr. (1996). pp. 82–83.

[142] Adapted from Swidoll, C. (1987). *The quest for character.* Multnomah. https://www.christianitytoday.com/pastors/1987/fall/8714038.html.

[143] Stanley, A., (2017, December 18). *The "Wow" and the "How".* Global Leadership Summit. https://globalleadership.org/videos/leading-organizations/the-wow-and-the-how

[144] MacInnis, A., (2020, December 21). COVID-19 Hurts. But the Bible Brings Hope. *Christianity Today.* https://www.christianitytoday.com/ct/2021/january-february/bible-hope-covid19-flourishing-study.html. For more on Harvard's Human Flourishing Program, see https://hf-

h.fas.harvard.edu/about. For more on the impact of religious communities on human flourishing, see https://hfh.fas.harvard.edu/religious-communities.

[145] Louw, J. P., & Nida, E. A. (1996). p. 675–677.

[146] Adapted from Batterson, M., (2020). *Win the day: 7 daily habits to help you stress less & accomplish more.* Multnomah. pp. 26-27.

[147] (2017, May 13) Roots of Adventure, *Vancouver Sun*; https://www.pressreader.com/

[148] Inklings (1985). *Christianity Today / Christian History.* https://www.christianitytoday.com/history/issues/issue-7/inklings.html

[149] Britt, R. R. (2019, August 27). *Optimists live longer.* Elemental. https://elemental.medium.com/optimists-live-longer-e0607686d58b

[150] Arichea, D. C., & Nida, E. A. (1980). *A handbook on the first letter from Peter.* United Bible Societies. p. 140.

[151] Michaels, J. R. (1988). *1 Peter (Vol. 49)* (Metzger, B. M., Hubbard, D. A., & Barker, G. W., general editors). Word, Incorporated. pp. 247-249.

[152] Vine, W. E., Unger, M. F., & White, W., Jr. (1996). pp. 312.

[153] Hammock, M. L. (1988) Other women of the early church. *Christian History, Issue 17.* https://christianhistoryinstitute.org/magazine/article/women-of-early-church-gallery

[154] (2017, July 27). *1 in 4 people entertain guests at home either daily or weekly.* Growth from Knowledge. https://www.gfk.com/press/1-in-4-people-entertain-guests-at-home-either-daily-or-weekly.

[155] Poggioli, S., (2020, April 7). *In Naples, pandemic 'solidarity baskets' help feed the homeless.* WNPR. https://www.wnpr.org/post/naples-pandemic-solidarity-baskets-help-feed-homeless.

[156] Golliver, B., (2020, January 29). Los Angeles is still grieving and still can't believe that it lost Kobe Bryant. *The Washington Post.* https://www.washingtonpost.com/sports/2020/01/28/kobe-bryant-los-angeles-vigils/.

[157] Ibid.

[158] Chesterton, G. K., (1874-1936). https://www.forbes.com/quotes/3281/

[159] Vine, W. E., Unger, M. F., & White, W., Jr. (1996). p. 264.

[160] Goel, V. R. (2021, March 15) *Yo-Yo Ma brought his cello with him to get his COVID-19 shot — and then played a surprise concert.* CBS News. https://www.cbsnews.com/news/yo-yo-ma-covid-19-vaccine-cello-surprise-concert/. You can see a clip of this event here: https://www.youtube.com/watch?v=4FC0-NRN-vDM.

[161] Young, R., and McMahon, S. (2020, March 26) *Cello maestro Yo-Yo Ma provides musical solace.* WBUR. https://www.wbur.org/hereandnow/2020/03/26/yo-yo-ma-songs-of-comfort

[162] Vine, W. E., Unger, M. F., & White, W., Jr. (1996). pp. 410.

[163] O'Keefe, P. A., Dweck, C. S., Walton, G. M., (2018, October) Implicit theories of interest: Finding your passion or developing it? *Psychological Science.* https://www.ncbi.nlm.nih.gov/pmc/articles/PMC6180666/

[164] Brooks, D., (2011, May 30). It's not about you. *New York Times.* https://www.nytimes.com/2011/05/31/opinion/31brooks.html

[165] Bachelder, Cheryl (2015) *Dare to serve: How to drive superior results by serving others.* Berrett-Koehler Publishers

[166] Parrish, K. (2013) *No cape required.* Thomas Nelson. pp. 31-32

[167] Vine, W. E., Unger, M. F., & White, W., Jr. (1996).. p. 276.

[168] Louw, J. P., & Nida, E. A. (1996). p. 476.

[169] Vine, W. E., Unger, M. F., & White, W., Jr. (1996). p. 276.

[170] Arichea, D. C., & Nida, E. A. (1980). *A handbook on the first letter from Peter.* United Bible Societies. p. 141.

[171] Swindler, S., (2020, March 28) Columbia sportswear

ceo Tim Boyle cuts own salary to $10K, retail employees receive regular pay. *The Oregonian.* https://www.oregonlive.com/coronavirus/2020/03/columbia-sportswear-ceo-tim-boyle-cuts-own-salary-to-10k-retail-employees-receive-regular-pay.html

[172] Walker, S., (2017, May 12). The seven leadership secrets of great team captains. *The Wall Street Journal.* https://www.wsj.com/articles/the-seven-leadership-secrets-of-great-team-captains-1494595600. See also, Walker, S., (2017), *The Captain Class.* Random House.

[173] Vine, W. E., Unger, M. F., & White, W., Jr. (1996). p. 177

[174] O'Kane, C. (2020, February 13). *A couple flying home with their newly adopted daughter received an impromptu baby shower on the plane.* CBS News. https://www.cbsnews.com/news/a-couple-flying-home-with-their-newly-adopted-daughter-received-an-impromptu-baby-shower-on-the-plane/

[175] This story is adapted from Vogel, S. (2003, October 2) Tomb guards stand sentinel through Isabel's threatening sweep. *The Washington Post.* https://www.washingtonpost.com/archive/local/2003/10/02/tomb-guards-stand-sentinel-through-isabels-threatening-sweep/87319d69-e23e-4a0a-a75c-e9a2549d1a02/.

[176] Vine, W. E., Unger, M. F., & White, W., Jr. (1996). p. 16

[177] Louw, J. P., & Nida, E. A. (1996). p. 292.

[178] Strong, J. (2009). *A concise dictionary of the words in the Greek testament and the Hebrew bible (Vol. 1).* Logos Bible Software. P. 75. Newman, B. M., & Nida, E. A. (1973). *A handbook on Paul's letter to the Romans.* United Bible Societies. p. 239. Dunn, J. D. G. (1988). *Romans 9–16 (Vol. 38B).* (Metzger, B. M., Hubbard, D. A., & Barker, G. W., general editors). Word, Incorporated. p. 740.

[179] (2019, January 25), People: clinging to stardom by a finger. *The Week.* p. 10. See also the Academy Award-winning documentary *Free Solo.* Chin, J. (Director). (2018) *Free Solo* [Film]. National Geographic Partners.

[180] Guinness, O., (2016) *Impossible people.* IVP Books.

[181] Brown, D. J., (2014), *The boys in the boat.* Penguin Books. pp. 161-162

[182] Vine, W. E., Unger, M. F., & White, W., Jr. (1996). p. 310.

[183] Newman, B. M., & Nida, E. A. (1973). *A handbook on Paul's letter to the Romans.* United Bible Societies. P. 239. Dunn, J. D. G. (1988). p. 741.

[184] Bakalian, L. Nishan, (1994), *Leadership, Vol. 15, (No. 2).*

[185] McDowell, Edwin, (1985, November 17). Officer who broke Japanese war codes gets belated honor, *New York Times,* Section 1, Page 1. https://www.nytimes.com/1985/11/17/us/officer-who-broke-japanese-war-codes-gets-belated-honor.html. See also, Layton, Edwin T. (1987) *"And I Was There": Pearl harbor and midway -- Breaking the Secrets.* William Morrow and Company.

[186] Mulligan, R. (1962). *To Kill a Mockingbird* [Film]. Universal Pictures. For this scene, see https://www.youtube.com/watch?v=q7CX_5D6y6E. Lee, H., (1960) *To Kill A Mockingbird.* J. B. Lippincott and Company.

4. Engaging Our Culture

[187] Migliore, D. L. (2014). pp. 276-278.

[188] Migliore, D. L. (2014). pp. 279-280.

[189] Schaeffer, K. (2021, January 28). *Racial, ethnic diversity increases yet again with the 117th Congress.* Pew Research Center. https://pewrsr.ch/3rdbdyr

[190] Stevenson, B. (2015) *Just mercy.* Spiegel & Grau. See also Stevenson, B (2012, March). *We need to talk about an injustice* [Video]. TED Conferences. https://youtu.be/c2tOp7OxyQ8. (23:41)

[191] Greer, S. (2021, January 19) *Can deep listening heal our divisions?* Greater Good Magazine. https://greatergood.berkeley.edu/article/item/can_deep_listening_heal_our_divisions.

[192] Brown, D., (2017, August 20) *How one man convinced 200 Ku Klux Klan mem-*

bers yo give up their robes. NPR. https://www.npr.org/2017/08/20/544861933/how-one-man-convinced-200-ku-klux-klan-members-to-give-up-their-robes.

[193] While not everyone will share each of Davis' starting points or perspectives, he does provide an example of spanning divides and listening. Ornstein, M. (Director). (2016). *Accidental courtesy: Daryl Davis, race & America* [Film]. Sound and Vision.

[194] https://www.biola.edu/blogs/winsome-conviction

[195] Hubbard, D. A., Fuller Theological Seminary, personal interaction, fall 1991.

[196] Diamant, J., (2021, February 19). *Three-quarters of Black Americans say Black churches have helped promote racial equality.* Pew Research Center. https://pewrsr.ch/3qI35Gk. See also the four-hour documentary series with Henry Louis Gates, Jr., *The Black Church.* https://www.pbs.org/show/black-church/

[197] One starting point for learning from the Black Church, and the way it has interpreted Scripture to sustain itself, is Esau McCaulley's personal and scholarly work *Reading While Black* (2020) from IVP Academic.

[198] https://braverangels.org/

[199] https://www.goodreads.com/quotes/7615413-to-love-is-to-will-the-good-of-the-other

[200] Northouse, P. (2021) *Leadership: Theory and Practice, 9th edition.* Sage Publications. pp. 2-7.

[201] Simpson, M., (2011, June 24) *New peace bridge is symbol of hope in 'stroke city'* BBC. https://www.bbc.com/news/uk-northern-ireland-foyle-west-13901885.

ABOUT THE AUTHOR

Derek Zahnd

Derek Zahnd, Ph.D. began serving churches in 1990 and now serves in the School of Theology and Leadership at William Jessup University in Rocklin, CA.

www.ingramcontent.com/pod-product-compliance
Ingram Content Group UK Ltd.
Pitfield, Milton Keynes, MK11 3LW, UK
UKHW021937190726
13853UKWH00004B/1507

9 798476 604877